Progressive Independence: Jazz

A Comprehensive Guide To Basic Jazz Drumming Technique

by Ron Spagnardi

Design and layout by Scott Bienstock

Printed in USA

Fifth Printing © 2017

Published By:
Modern Drummer Publications, Inc.
271 Route 46 West
Suite H-212
Fairfield, NJ 07004 USA

www.moderndrummer.com

CONTENTS

INTRODUCTION

The Power Of Coordinated Independence

In jazz drumming, "coordinated independence" refers to the ability to execute separate rhythms in each hand and foot in a *coordinated* manner, yet totally *independent* of one another. More specifically, it refers to the ability to execute various rhythmic figures on the snare and bass drum against an uninterrupted "time pattern" on the ride cymbal and hi-hat.

This ability is an essential part of jazz drumming. The greater your understanding and ability to develop this aspect of your playing, the more you'll be able to support and respond to what the players around you are doing in a musical and effective manner. The purpose of this book is to help you gain a substantial level of coordinated independence, and to free the snare drum hand and bass drum foot from the ride cymbal and hi-hat pattern.

At the early stages, expect to pay careful attention to the four separate parts of each exercise. Each part should be played *precisely* as written. Though this may prove somewhat difficult at first, with practice the ride cymbal and hi-hat pattern will begin to function on their own, with little or no conscious thought required. At that point, full attention can be devoted to the snare drum and bass drum figures. This takes some time, so be prepared to be patient.

Once the techniques in this book are mastered, you'll be able to play rhythmic figures on the snare and bass drum in a "comping" style behind a jazz soloist, as well as accentuate ensemble figures in a big band situation without disrupting the time flow.

About This Book

The time pattern used throughout this book is the one most commonly used by jazz players. Though many variations exist in modern jazz performance (the author recommends *Creative Timekeeping* by Rick Mattingly, published by Hal Leonard, as a good source for developing coordinated independence against variations in the jazz time pattern), the pattern below is the *only* one we'll use to achieve our goal, and it is the foundation upon which everything else in this book is built:

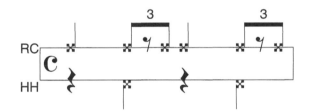

The format of this book is simple and straightforward. Each of the first three sections starts with a series of one-bar coordinated independence exercises, beginning with quarter notes and progressing through 8ths, syncopated figures, triplets, and triplet partials. The Summary Exercises that follow use a combination of the previous one-bar figures, and serve as a conclusion to each section.

Section I is devoted solely to snare drum independence, while Section II focuses on the bass drum. Section III offers the challenge of snare and bass drum combinations set against the ride cymbal and hi-hat pattern, and the six exercises in Section IV provide a summary to everything previously learned.

Getting The Most From This Book

1) All of the one-bar exercises should be repeated until all four parts fall comfortably between the limbs and until each can be played with a relaxed, musical feel.

2) Practice *slowly* and methodically at first, with a solid, steady time feel. *Do not* increase the tempo until each exercise is played accurately and smoothly. *Do not* move on to the next exercise until the previous one has been mastered.

3) Be certain you're comfortable with the one-bar exercises before attempting the twenty-four-bar Summary Exercises. Each Summary Exercise presents a considerable challenge and should ultimately be played straight through from beginning to end at a comfortable tempo.

4) *All* 8th-note figures and syncopated rhythms *must* be played with a "jazz interpretation," whereby a measure of 8th notes, though written like this:

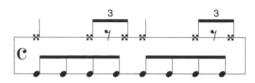

is played as "swung" 8th notes, in accordance with the triplet feel of the time pattern, like this:

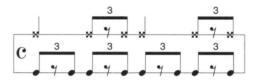

5)

Phrasing is a very important element of the swing feel, and accomplished through the use of subtle accents. As a very general rule, slightly accent all quarter notes and any 8th notes that are not immediately followed by other notes of any duration. Note how this "rule" applies in the following example:

6) Take ample time with Section II; this is the section that focuses on the bass drum. Rarely does the foot react as efficiently as the hand, so take each exercise *slowly* and focus on accuracy. As a side benefit, the exercises in Section II will help you develop greater foot strength, endurance, and control.

7) Practice with a metronome or drum machine to ensure a steady time flow.

8) *Sing* each snare and bass drum figure as you play, either out loud or to yourself. This greatly aids in mastering the coordination and helps achieve a more musical feel.

9) *Listen* to the many great small group and big band jazz drummers from the mid-'40s to the present who have effectively used coordinated independence. Although there are probably as many subtle variations in the interpretation of the jazz feel as there are great jazz drummers, to get you started I recommend checking out recordings with drumming by Max Roach, Roy Haynes, Art Blakey, Philly Joe Jones, Buddy Rich, Shelly Manne, Jimmy Cobb, Elvin Jones, Jack DeJohnette, and Tony Williams.

10) The expert guidance of a qualified instructor is highly recommended.

The following abbreviations are used throughout:

RC = Ride Cymbal   **SD** = Snare Drum   **BD** = Bass Drum   **HH** = Hi-Hat

SECTION I: SNARE DRUM INDEPENDENCE

PART 1: QUARTER-NOTE PATTERNS

The following fifteen exercises will help you develop a feel for playing straight quarter notes with the standard time beat. Be certain that you're playing all four parts of each exercise precisely as written. Repeat each exercise as many times as necessary until you can play it smoothly and accurately.

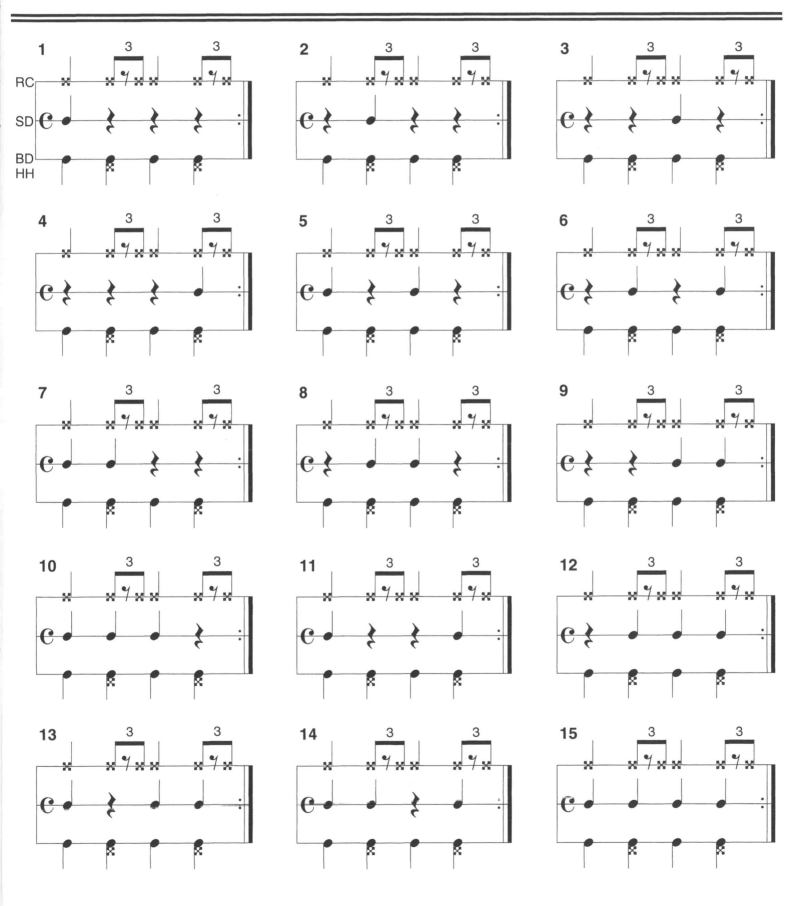

SUMMARY EXERCISE 1

This Summary Exercise (and all that follow) serves as a review of the previously learned material. Practice slowly at first, straight through from beginning to end, with an accurate, steady time flow. Go back and review the individual exercises if you encounter any problems with a particular measure or section of any of the Summary Exercises.

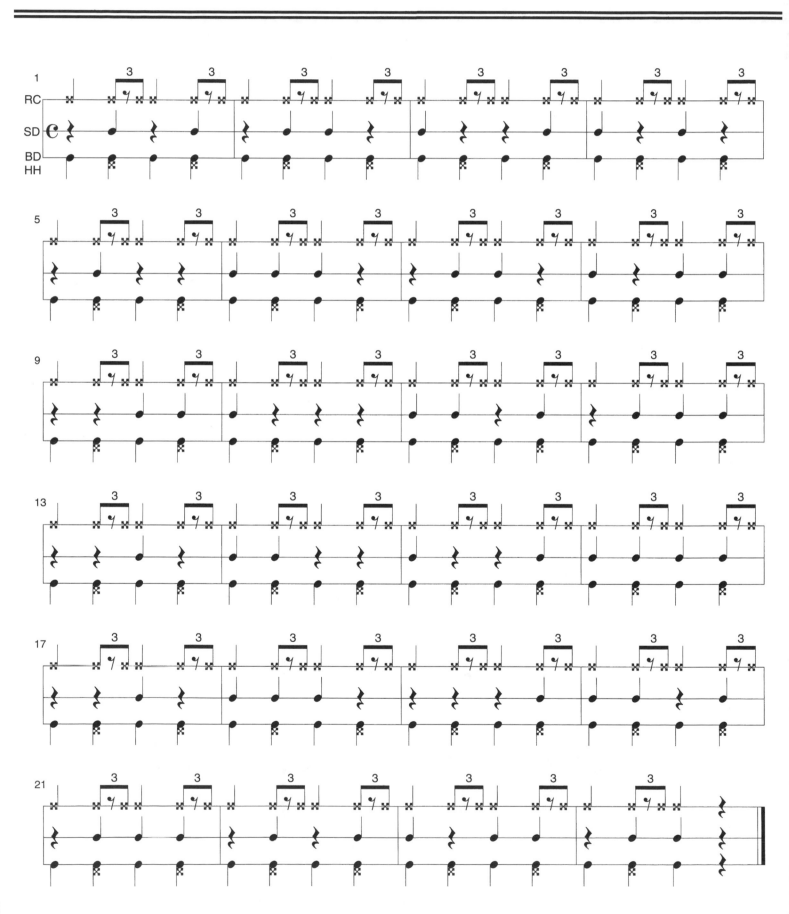

SUMMARY EXERCISE 2

PART 2: 8TH-NOTE PATTERNS

The following eight pages of material utilize 8th notes, 8th-note rests, and quarter notes in the snare drum hand. Remember that all 8th-note figures are to be played with a "jazz interpretation." Therefore, 8th notes written under the time pattern as straight 8th notes will *always* be played with a triplet (swing) feel, in accordance with the triplet feel of the time pattern.

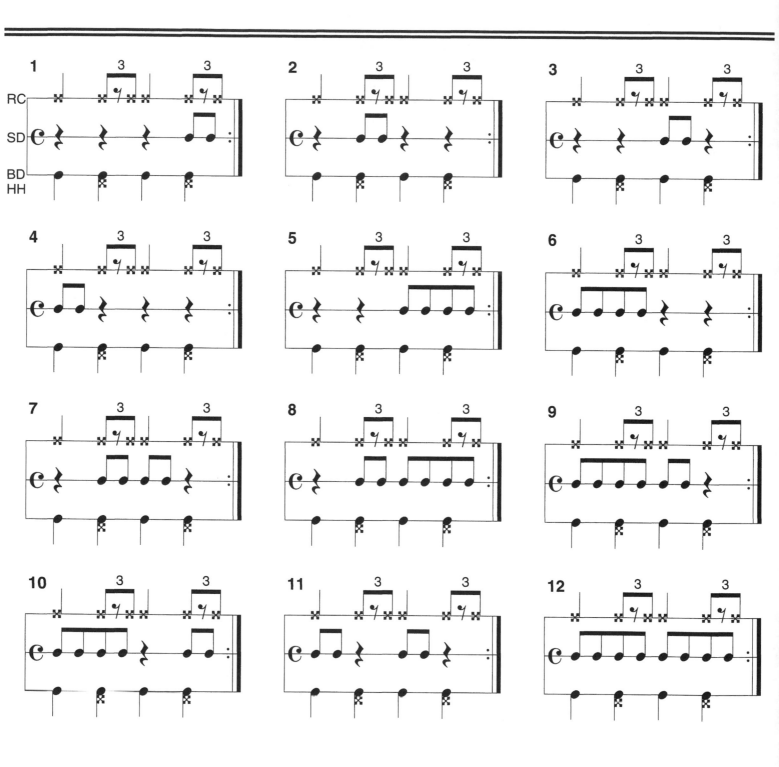

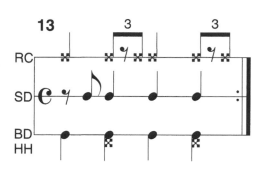

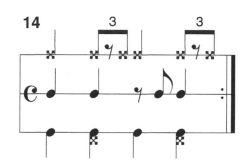

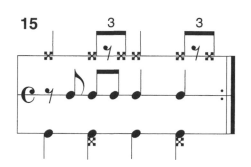

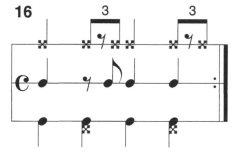

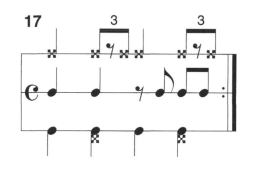

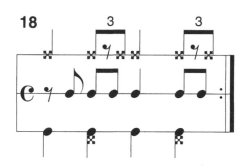

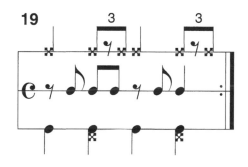

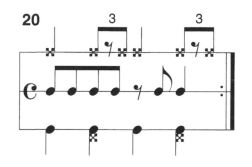

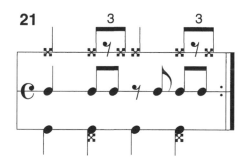

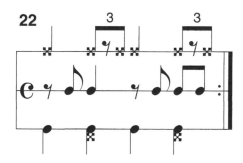

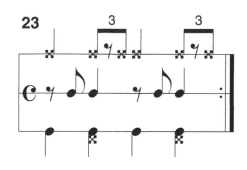

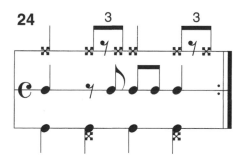

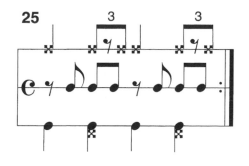

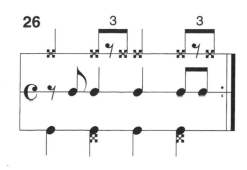

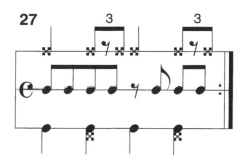

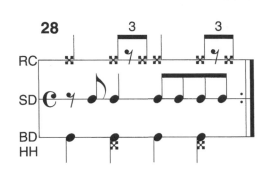

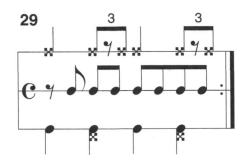

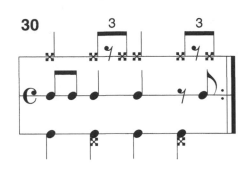

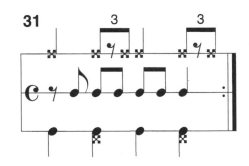

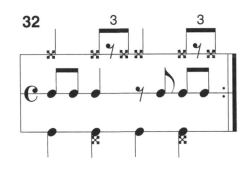

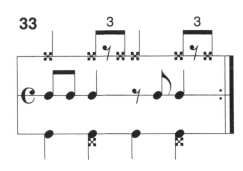

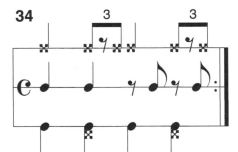

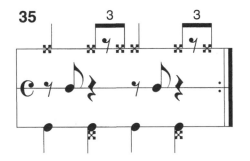

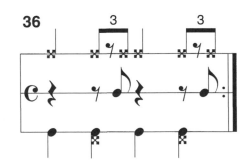

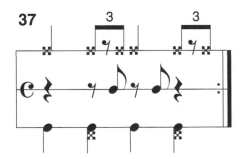

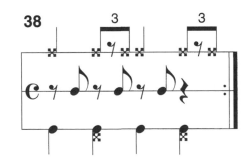

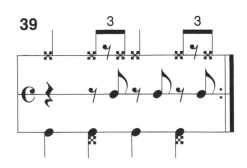

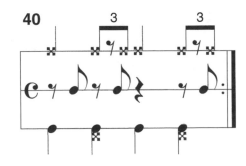

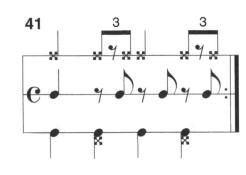

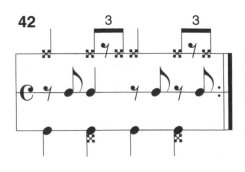

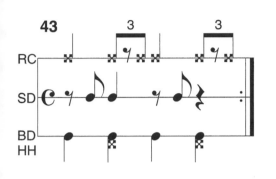

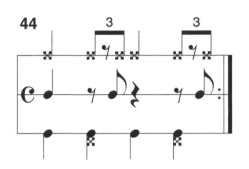

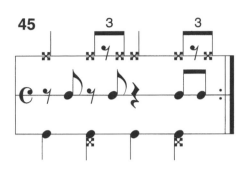

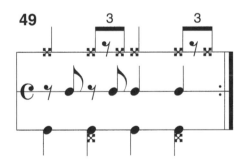

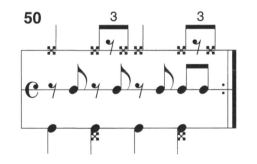

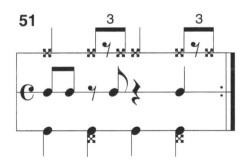

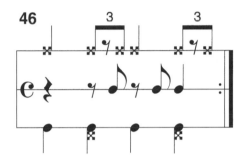

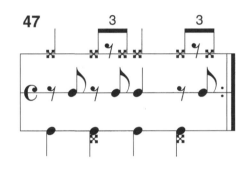

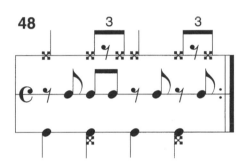

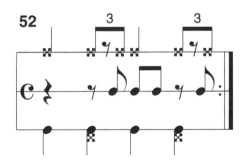

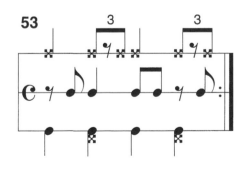

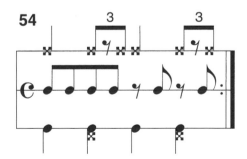

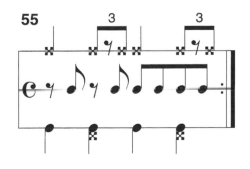

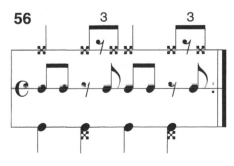

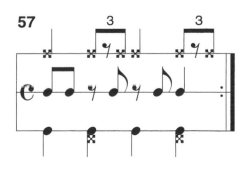

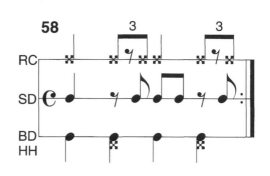

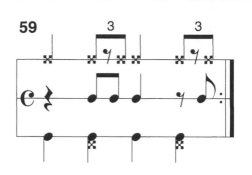

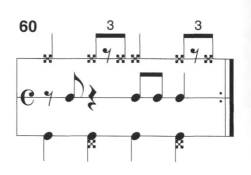

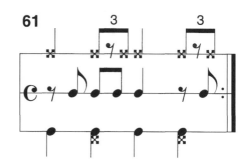

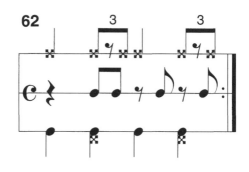

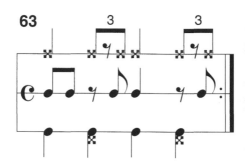

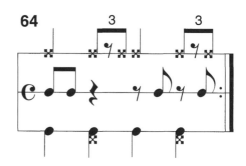

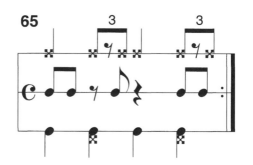

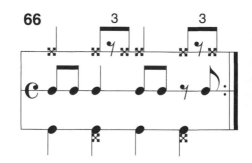

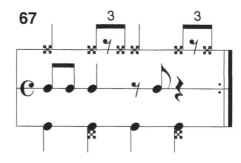

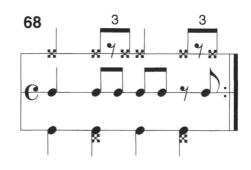

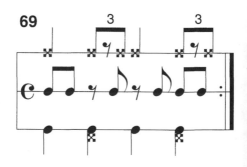

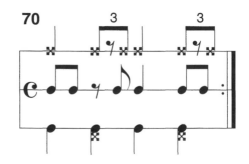

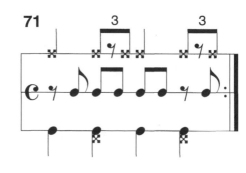

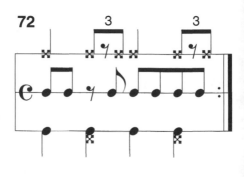

SUMMARY EXERCISE 3

SUMMARY EXERCISE 4

SUMMARY EXERCISE 5

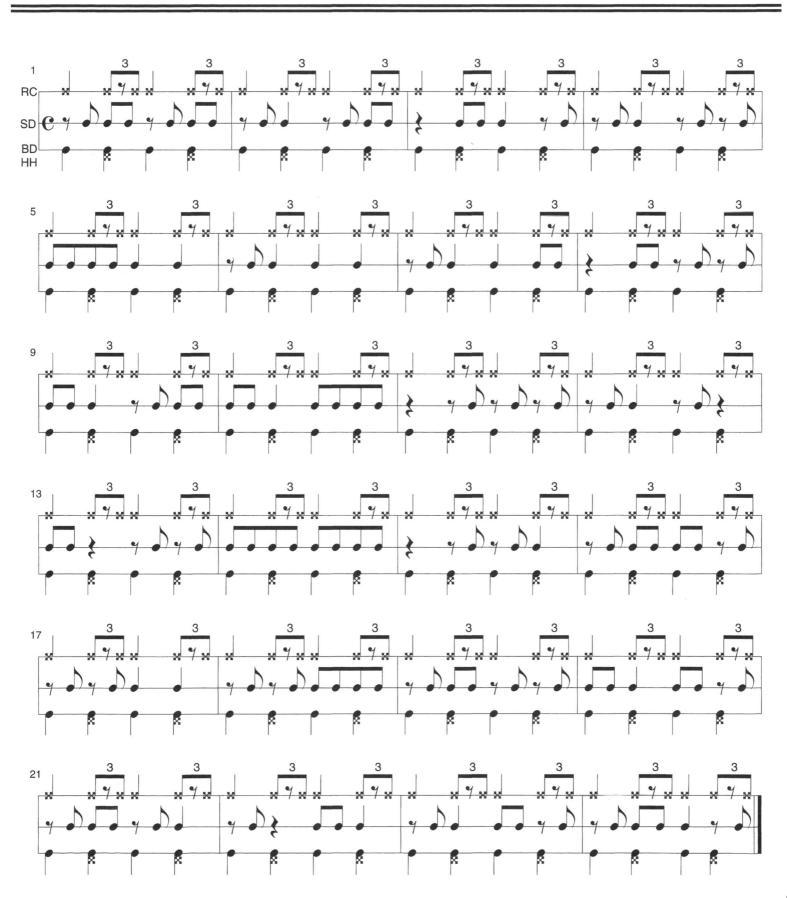

PART 3: SYNCOPATED PATTERNS

Though notated differently, the syncopated rhythms in Part 3 will sound the same as the 8th-note patterns previously covered, and are not likely to present any new independence problems. Syncopated notation is presented since this is how you're likely to see figures notated on a typical drum chart. As with the previous section on 8th notes, all syncopated rhythms should be played as "swung" 8th notes with a jazz feel.

Once you've mastered the basic independence of each exercise, for a more authentic jazz feel, try slightly accenting all the quarter notes and any 8th note that is not immediately followed by another note. This slight adjustment in phrasing will give the exercises a more relaxed swing feel common to the small group and big band jazz idioms.

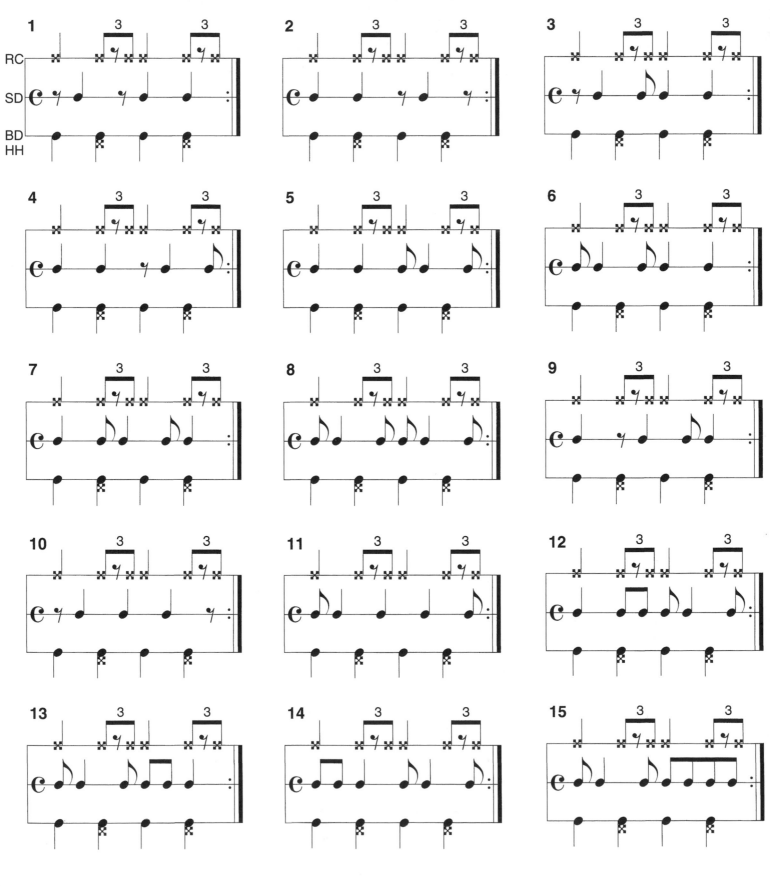

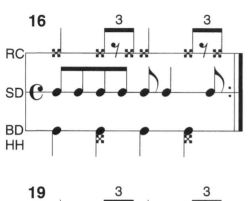

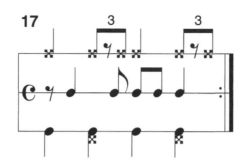

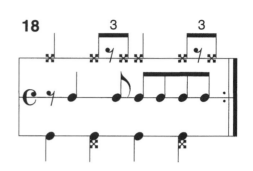

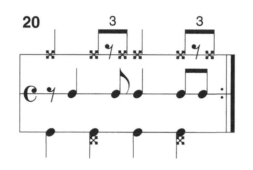

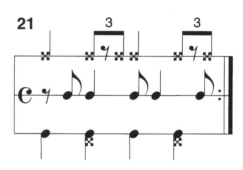

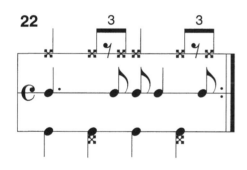

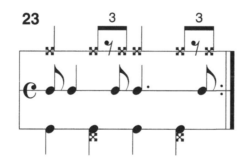

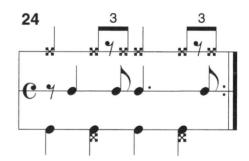

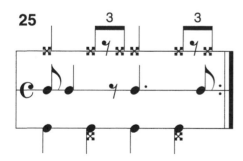

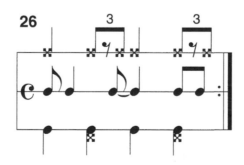

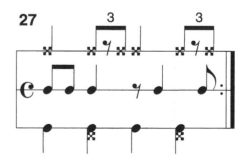

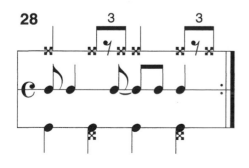

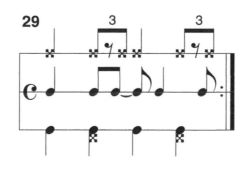

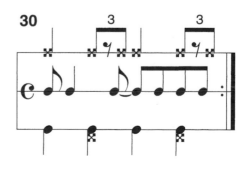

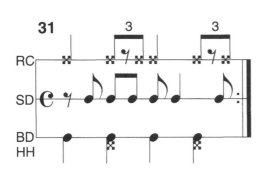

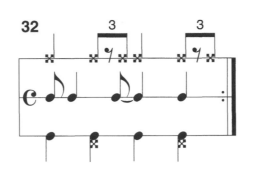

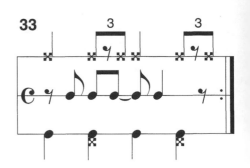

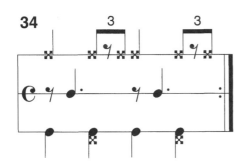

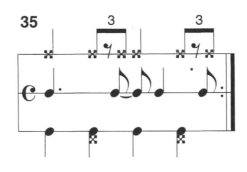

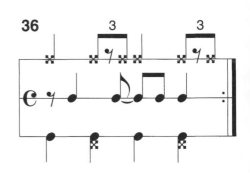

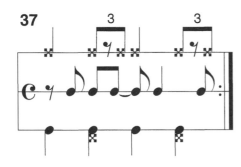

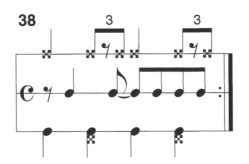

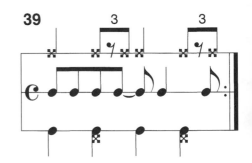

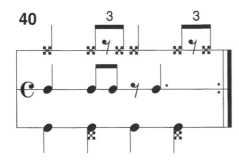

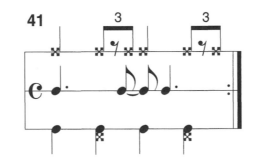

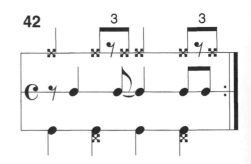

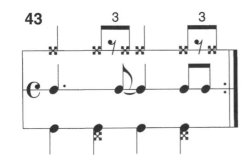

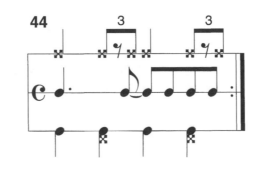

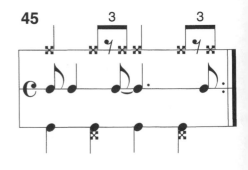

SUMMARY EXERCISE 6

SUMMARY EXERCISE 7

PART 4: TRIPLET PATTERNS

Developing a relaxed, natural triplet feel against the time pattern is an essential aspect of jazz drumming. Be careful not to rush the time when the triplet occurs on beats 2 and 4 in the snare drum part. Take each exercise slowly, and strive for accurate placement of all snare drum notes against the time beat.

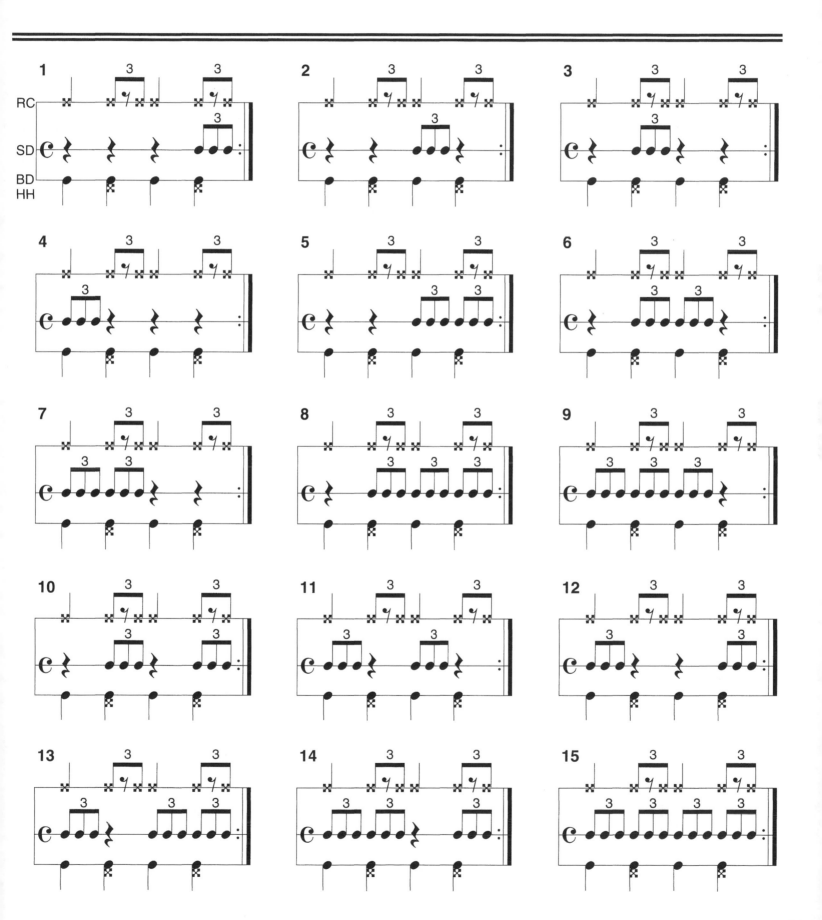

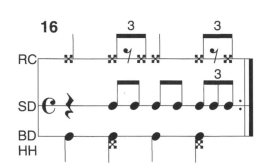
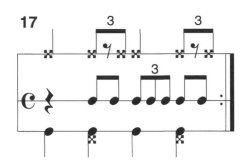
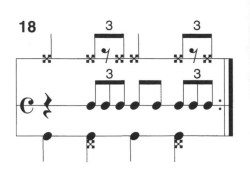

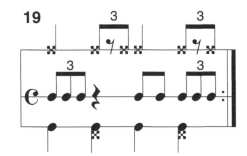
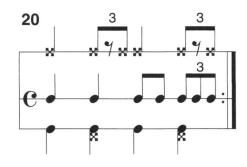
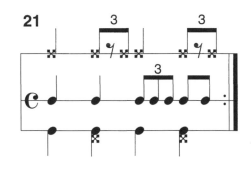

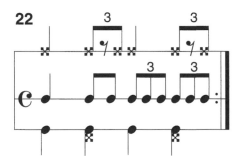
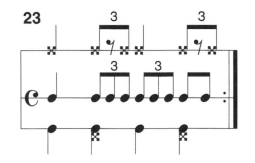
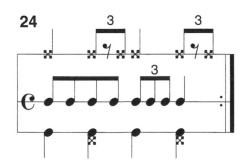

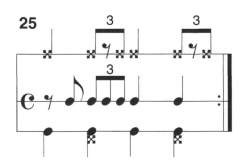
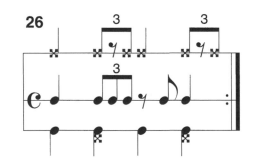
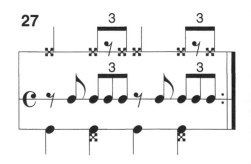

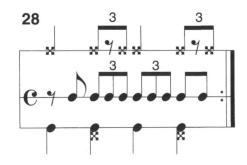
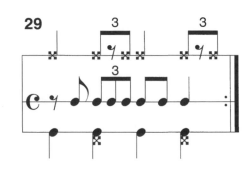
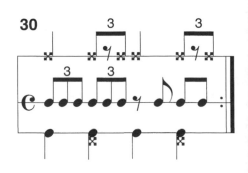

31

RC
SD
BD
HH

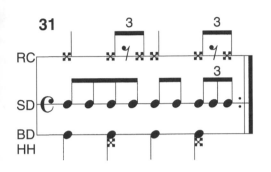

32

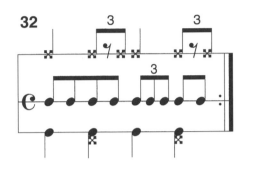

33

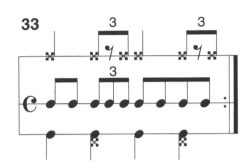

34

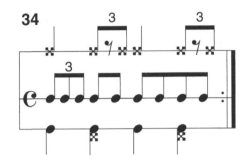

35

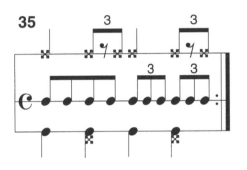

36

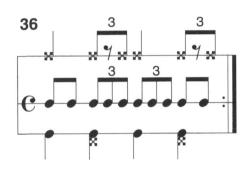

37

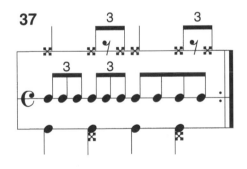

38

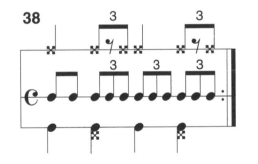

39

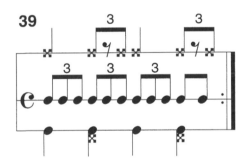

40

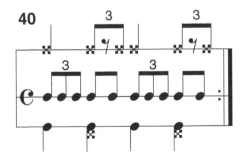

41

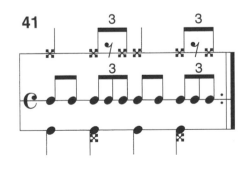

42

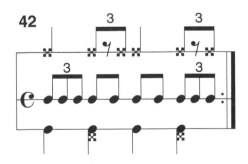

43

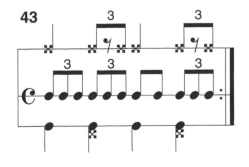

44

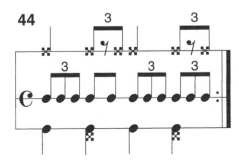

45

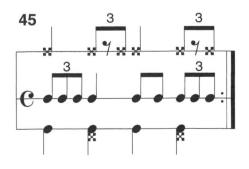

SUMMARY EXERCISE 8

SUMMARY EXERCISE 9

TRIPLET PARTIALS

The ninety individual exercises that follow involve the use of triplet partials—the three individual notes that make up the triplet group. In this book, the second partial is counted as "an" and the third partial is counted as "a." Exercises 1 through 15 begin with the second and third notes of the triplet against the time pattern. To add more "lift" to the feel of these exercises, try placing a bit more emphasis on the third partial, and keep the time loose and relaxed.

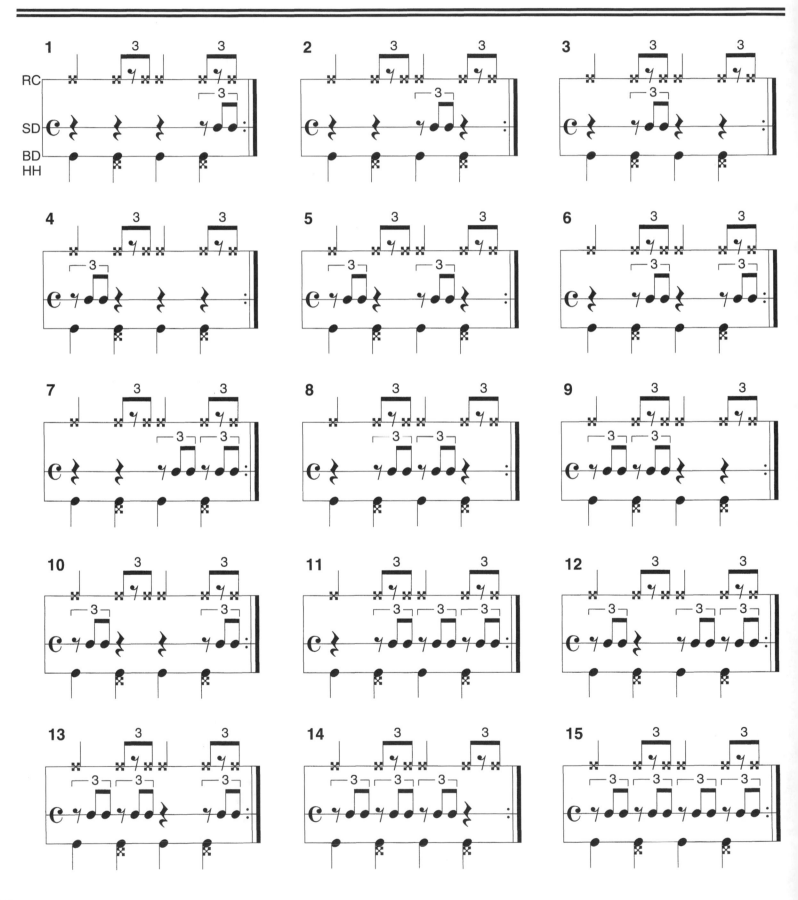

Note that the following exercises have the snare drum playing on the first and second partials of the triplet.

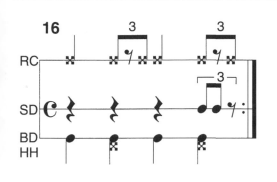

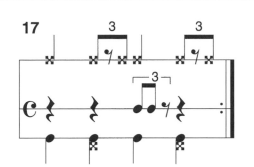

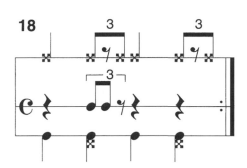

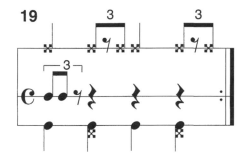

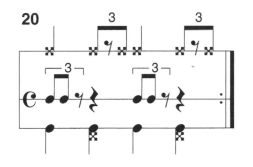

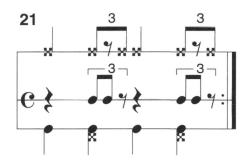

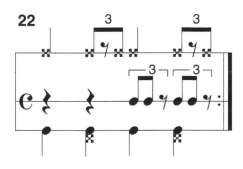

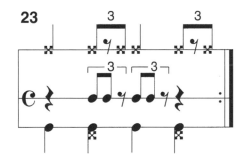

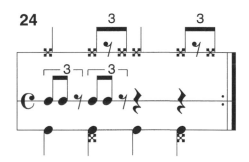

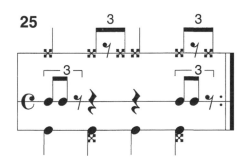

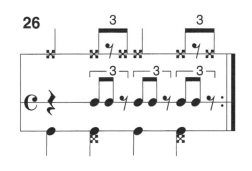

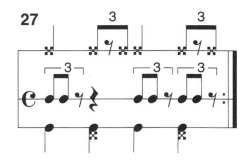

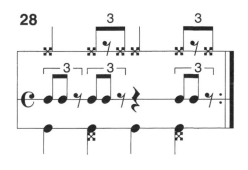

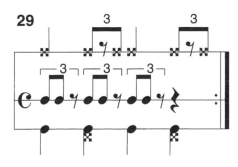

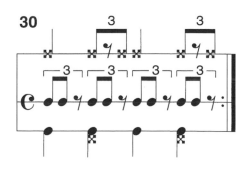

These exercises use the previous two triplet-partial combinations with the addition of 8th notes. Practice with a metronome to ensure a steady time feel.

31

RC
SD
BD
HH

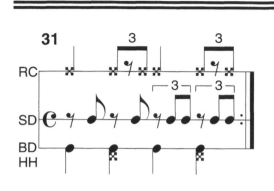

32

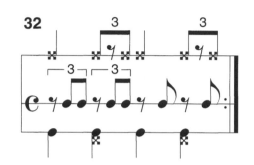

33

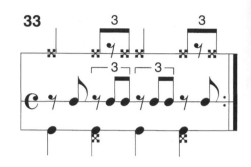

34

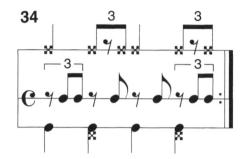

35

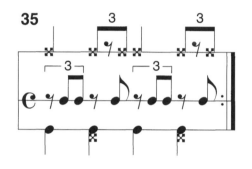

36

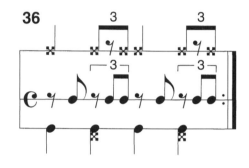

37

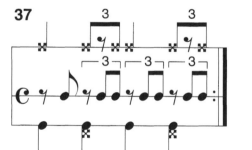

38

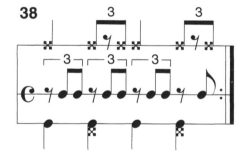

39

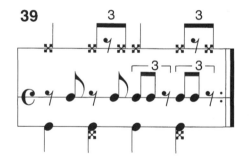

40

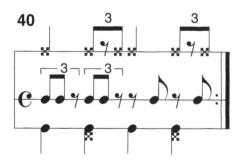

41

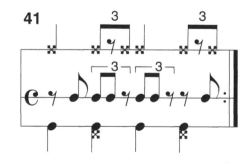

42

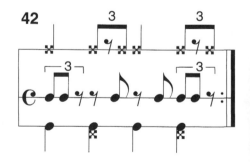

43

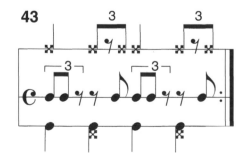

44

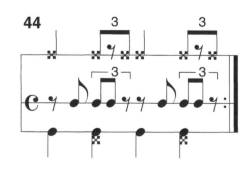

45

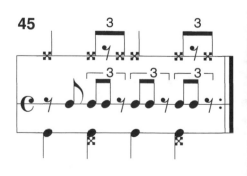

Playing the second partial of the triplet (exercises 47-57) is common in the jazz idiom, as is playing the first and third partials to produce the shuffle feel (exercise 58).

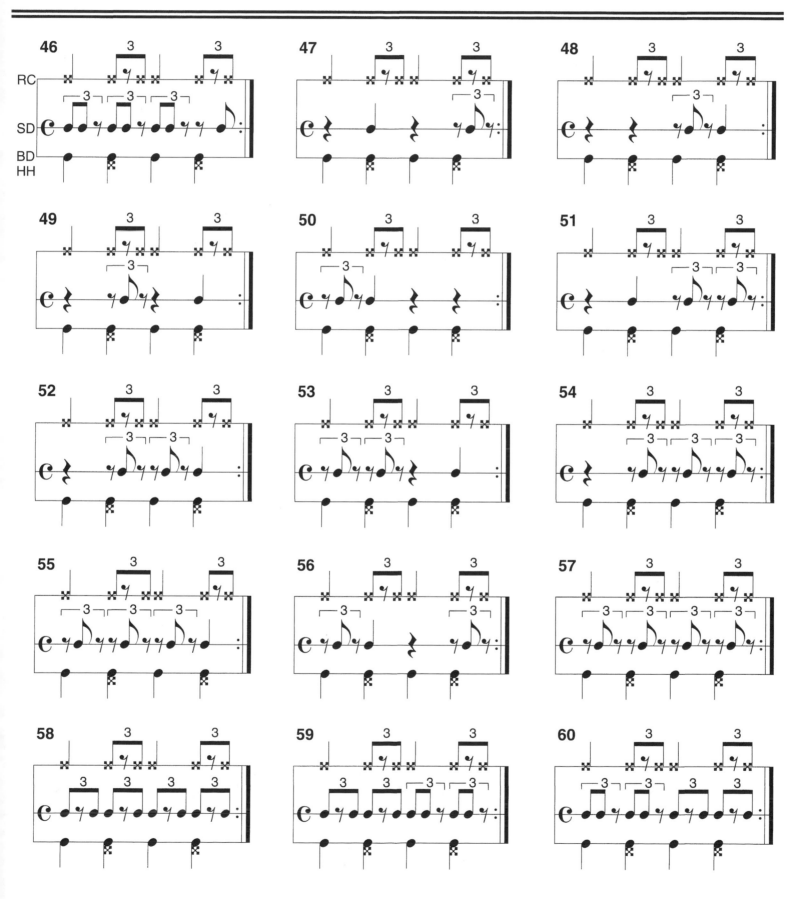

Exercises 61 through 75 utilize combinations of all the triplet partial rhythms covered thus far. Note the quarter-note-triplet feel that occurs in exercise 64, when the first and third partials of beat 3 and the second partial of beat 4 occur in sequence.

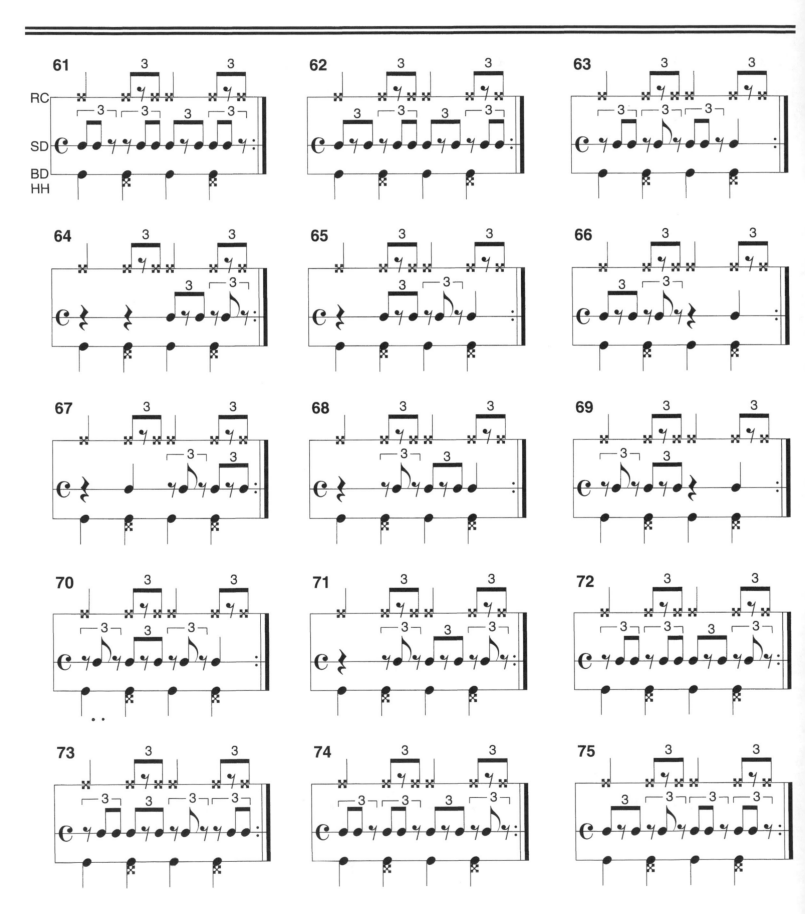

The various combinations of triplet partials on this page present both reading and independence challenges. For a more musical feel, try singing the snare drum rhythms as you play them.

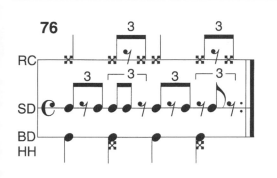

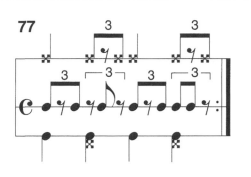

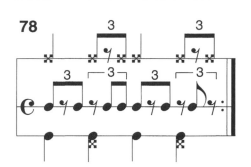

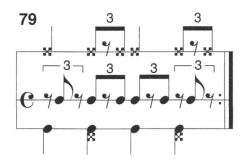

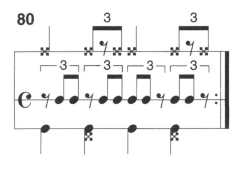

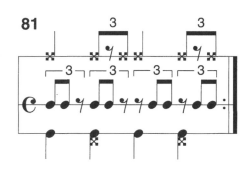

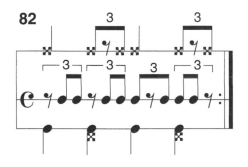

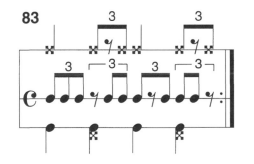

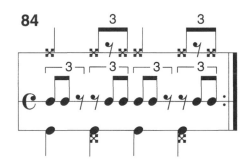

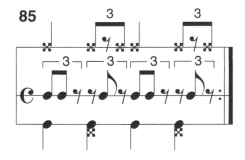

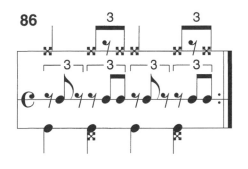

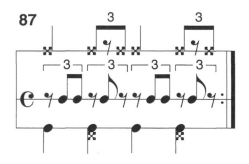

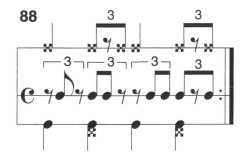

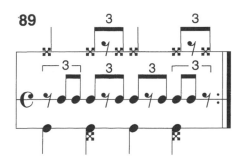

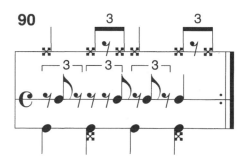

SUMMARY EXERCISE 10

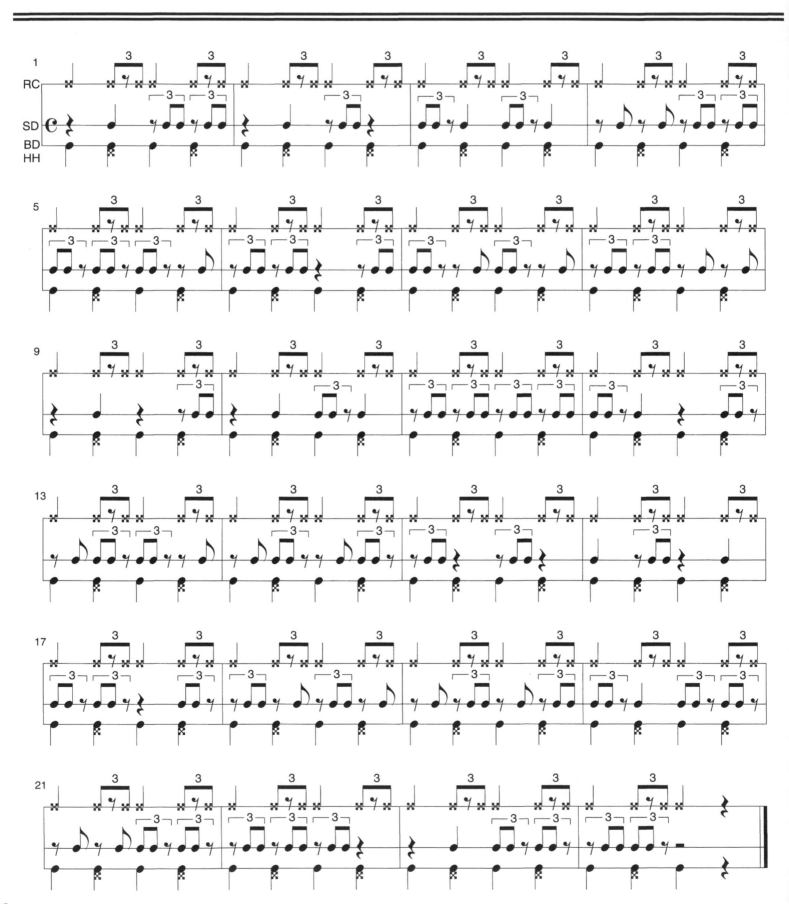

SUMMARY EXERCISE 11

SUMMARY EXERCISE 12

SECTION II: BASS DRUM INDEPENDENCE
PART 1: QUARTER-NOTE PATTERNS

Similar to Section I on snare drum independence, the bass drum independence section begins with quarter notes. As stated in the introduction, take your time with this section since the foot rarely reacts as quickly and as easily as the hand. Practice each exercise slowly and steadily and do not increase the speed until you're totally comfortable with each one.

SUMMARY EXERCISE 13

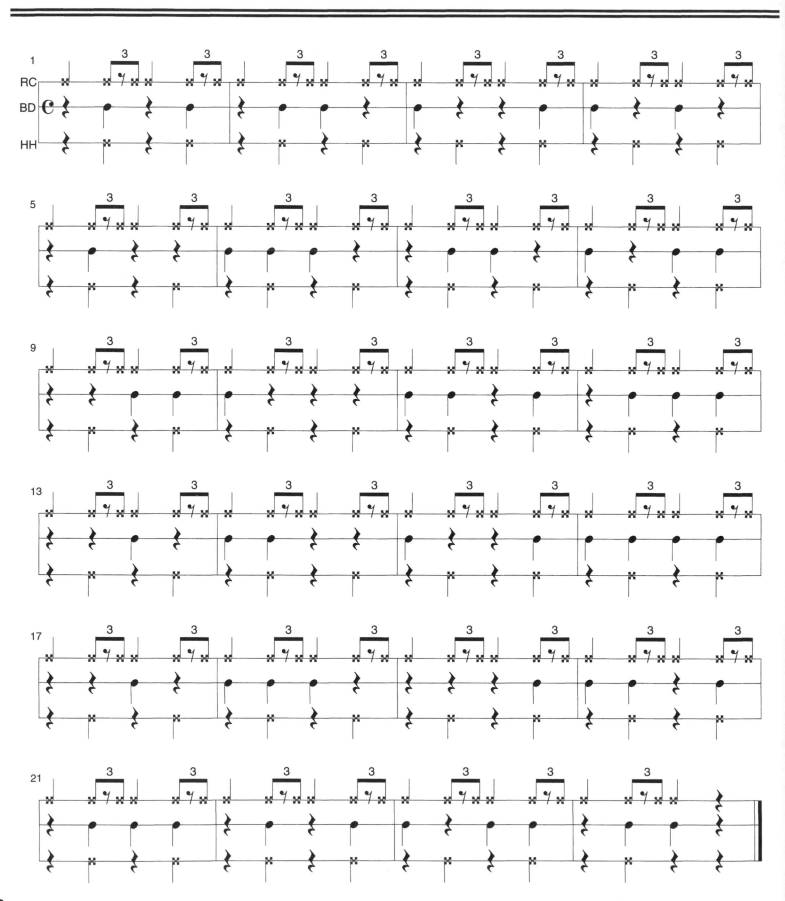

SUMMARY EXERCISE 14

PART 2: 8TH-NOTE PATTERNS

Eighth notes on the bass drum must also be played with a "jazz interpretation." Be sure the bass drum figures are accurately synchronized with the ride cymbal. A greater degree of strength and control of the bass drum foot will naturally develop with the dedicated practice of these exercises.

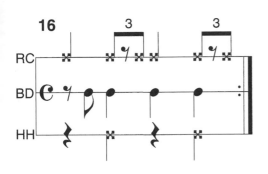
16

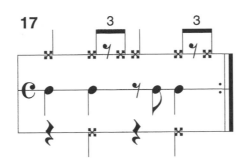
17

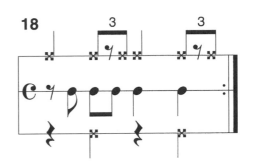
18

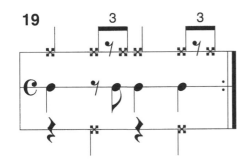
19

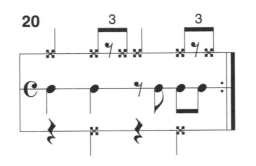
20

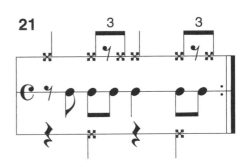
21

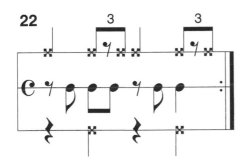
22

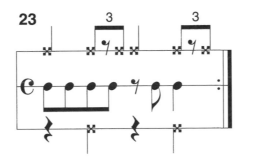
23

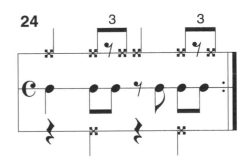
24

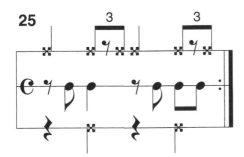
25

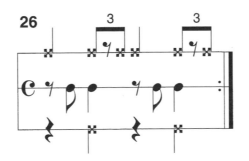
26

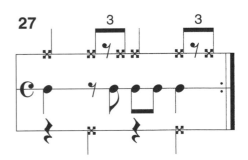
27

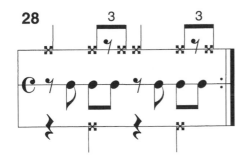
28

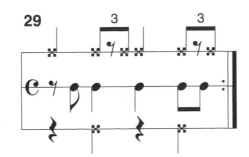
29

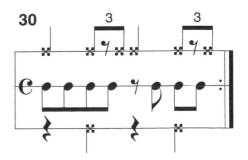
30

31

RC BD HH
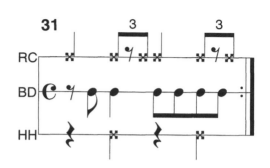

32
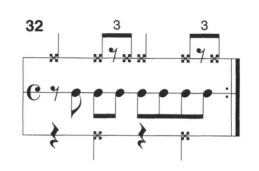

33
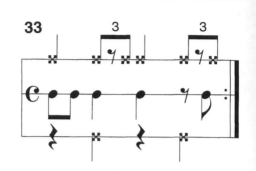

34
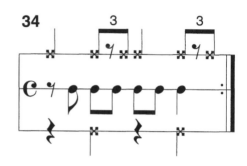

35
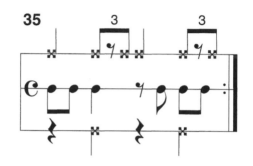

36
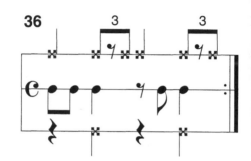

37
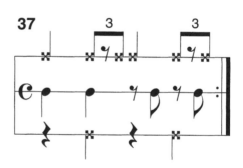

38
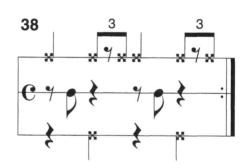

39
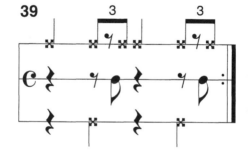

40
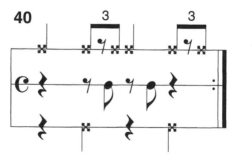

41
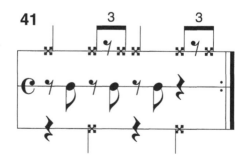

42
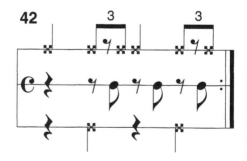

43
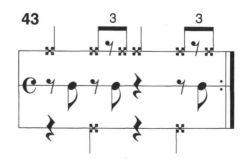

44
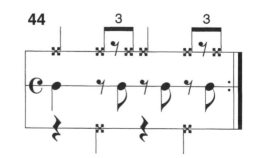

45
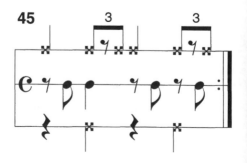

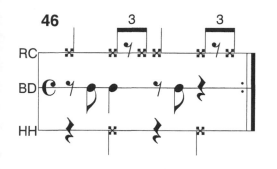

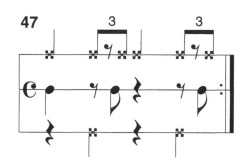

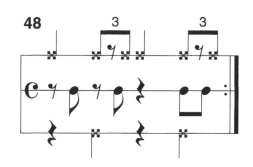

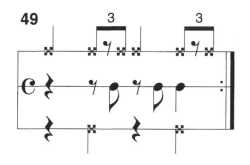

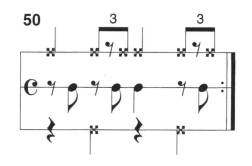

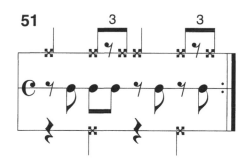

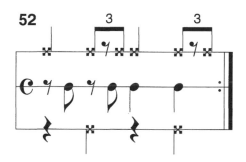

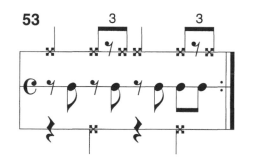

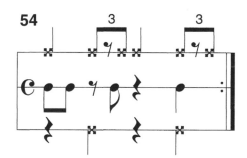

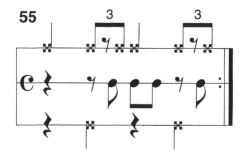

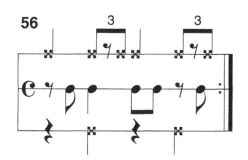

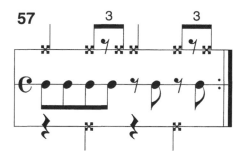

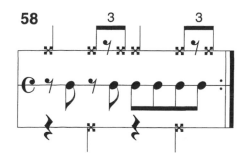

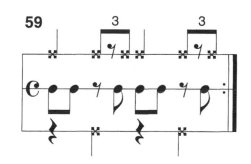

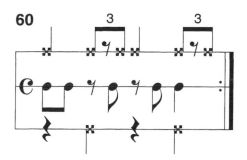

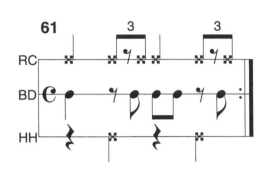

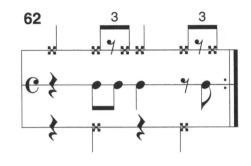

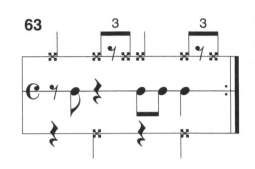

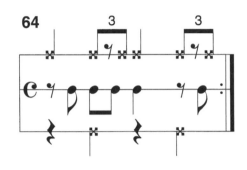

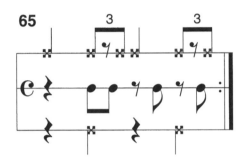

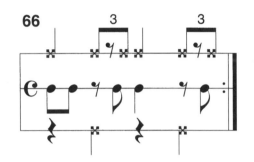

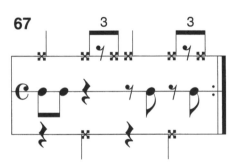

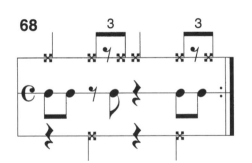

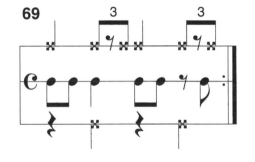

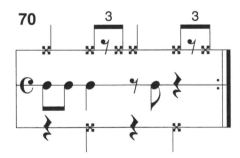

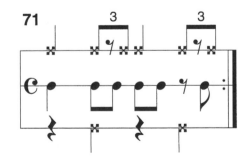

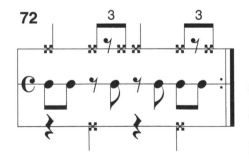

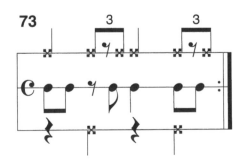

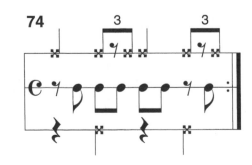

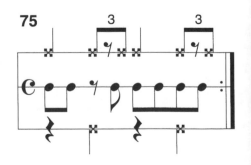

SUMMARY EXERCISE 15

SUMMARY EXERCISE 16

SUMMARY EXERCISE 17

PART 3: SYNCOPATED PATTERNS

Be certain you master all forty-five of the syncopated bass drum independence exercises that follow before attempting Summary Exercises 18 and 19.

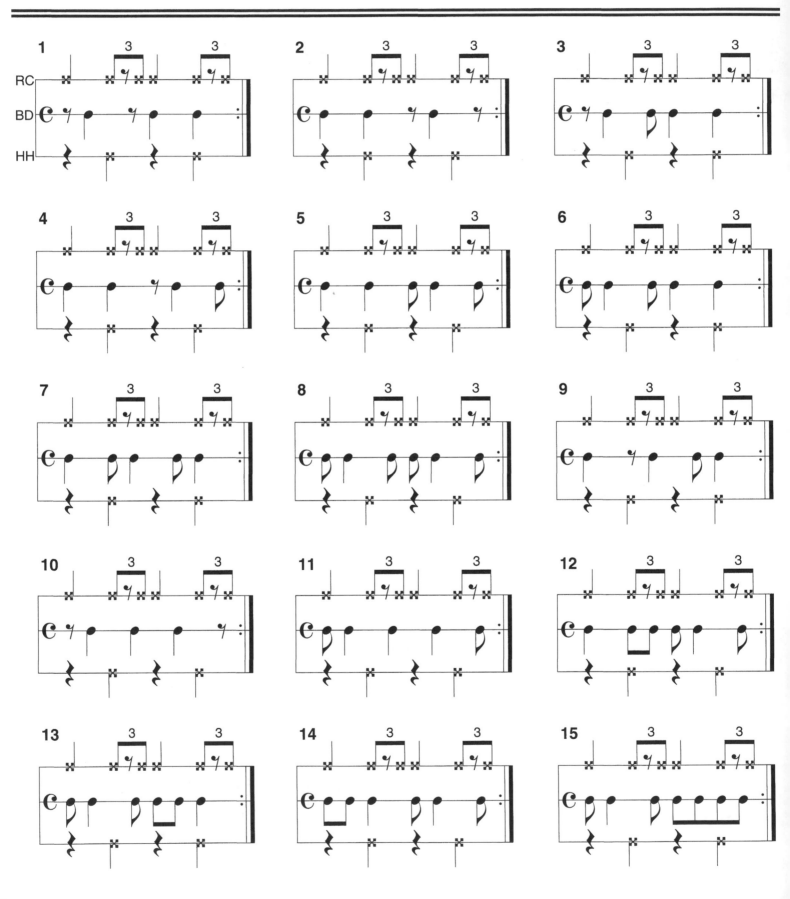

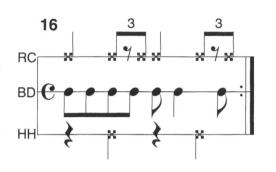

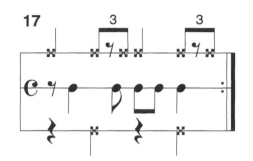

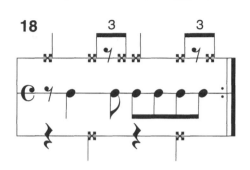

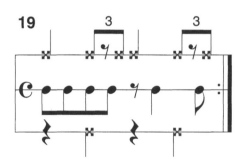

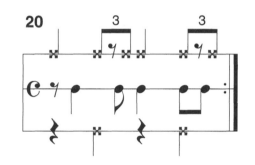

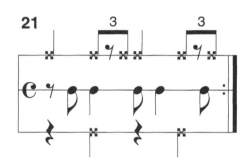

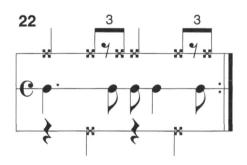

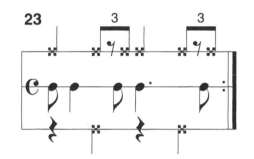

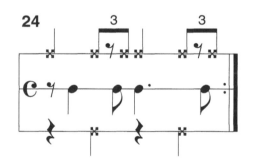

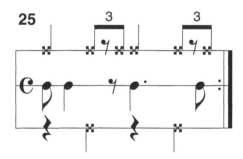

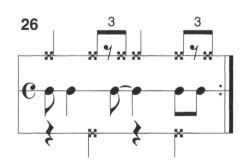

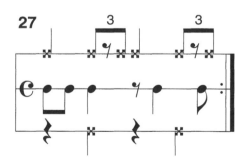

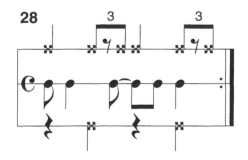

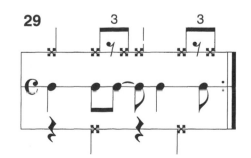

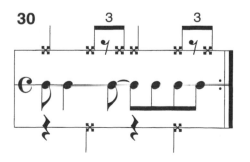

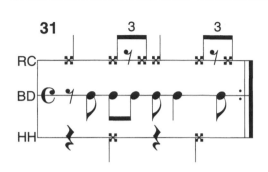

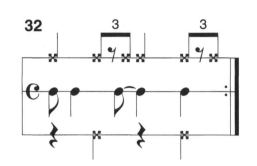

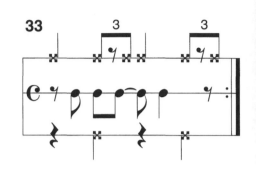

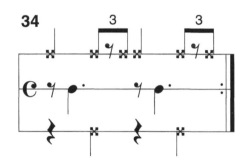

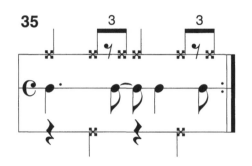

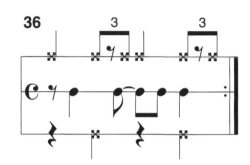

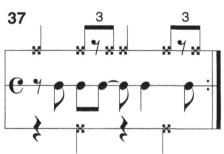

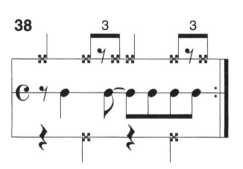

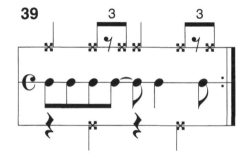

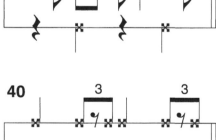

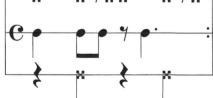

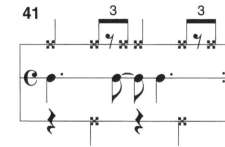

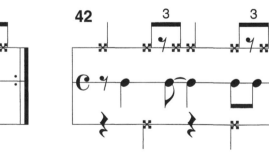

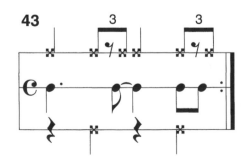

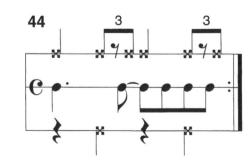

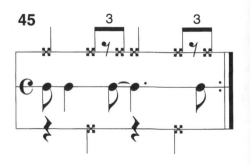

SUMMARY EXERCISE 18

SUMMARY EXERCISE 19

PART 4: TRIPLET PATTERNS

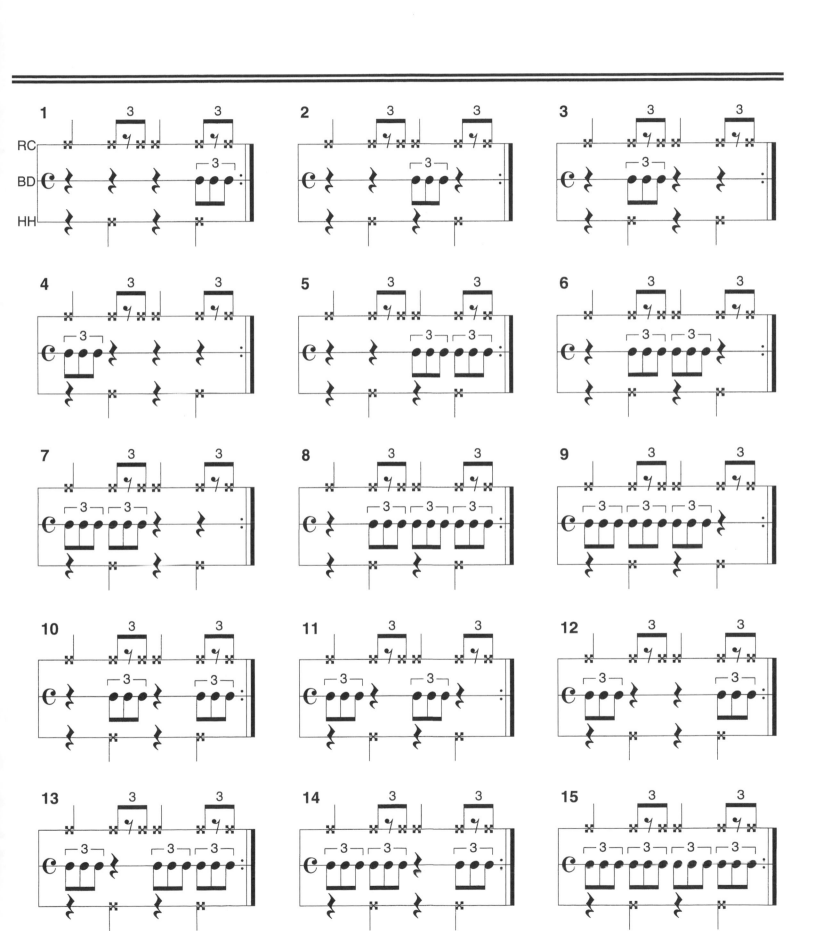

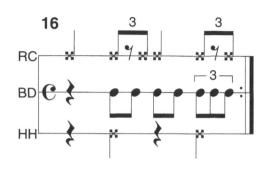

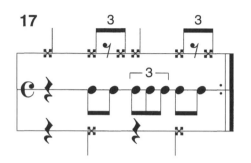

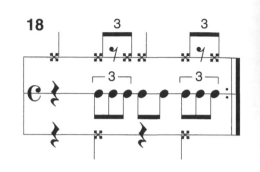

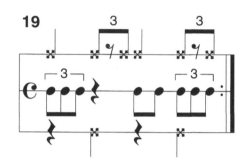

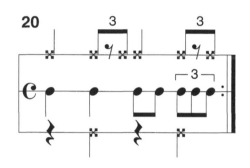

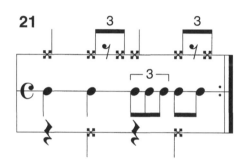

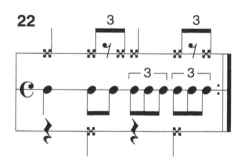

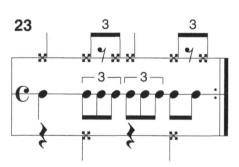

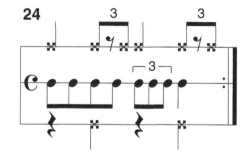

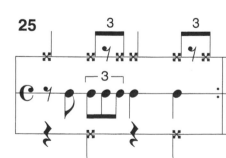

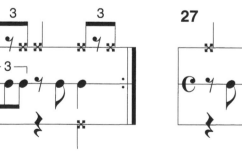

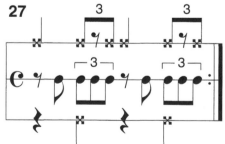

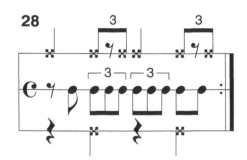

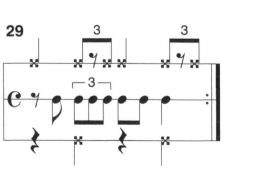

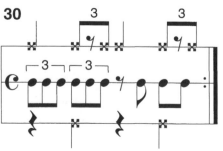

SUMMARY EXERCISE 20

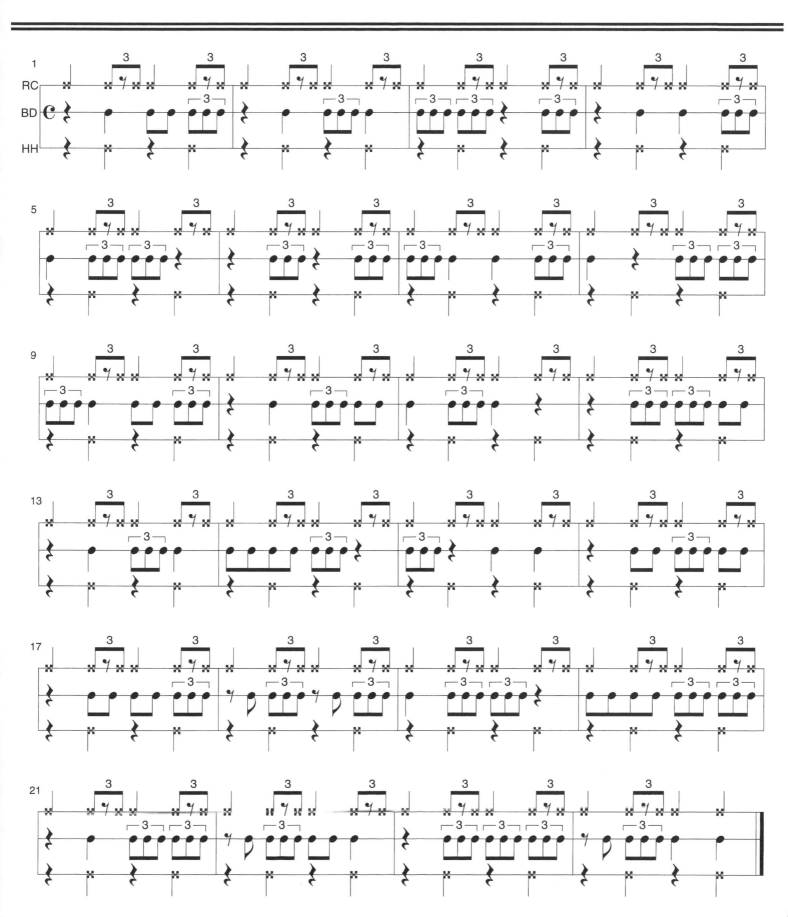

TRIPLET PARTIALS

The triplet partial rhythms that follow in the next seventy-five bass drum exercises are, for the most part, the same as those in the snare drum section. Be sure to focus on accuracy rather than speed. Control is the key goal here.

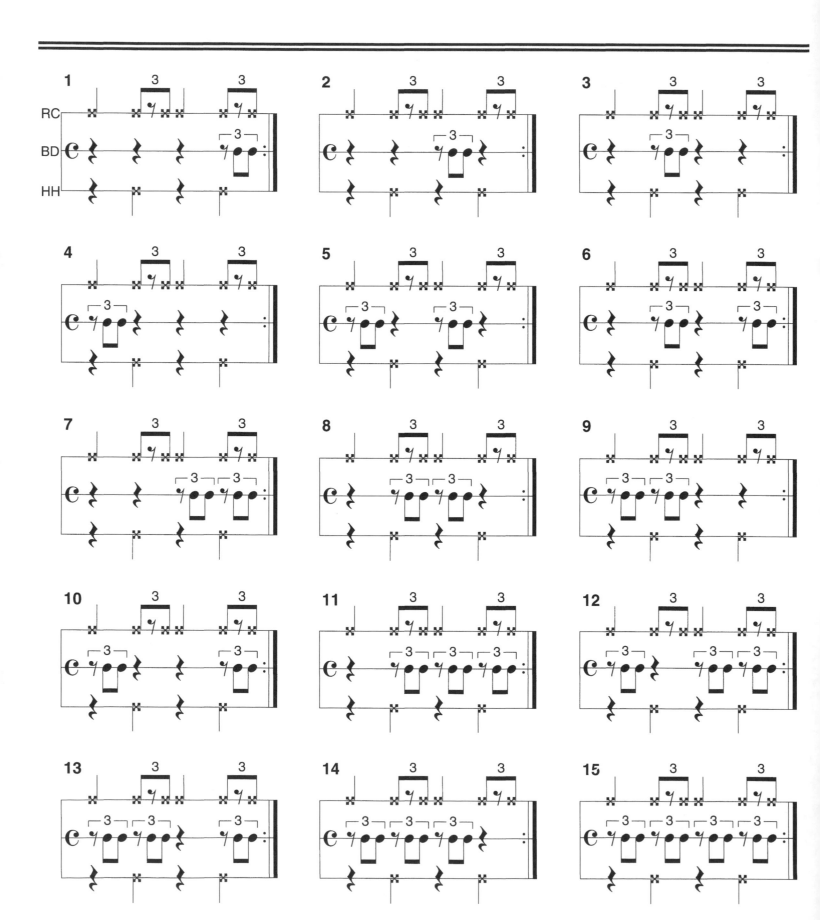

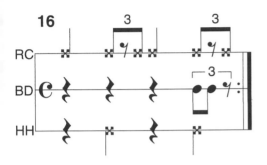

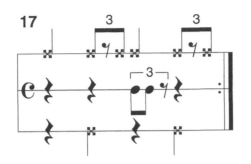

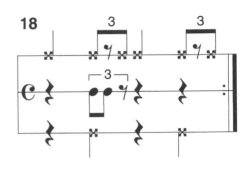

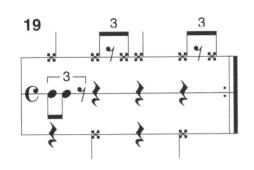

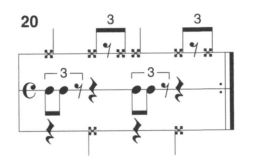

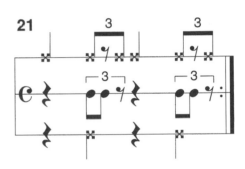

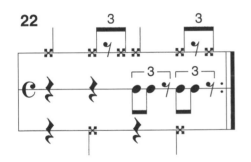

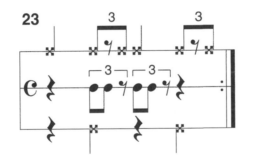

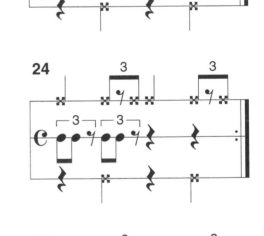

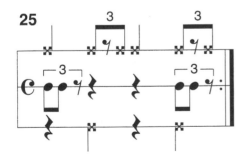

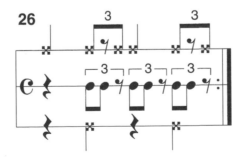

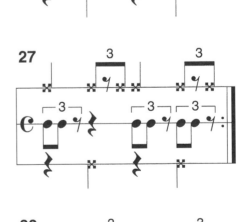

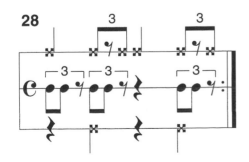

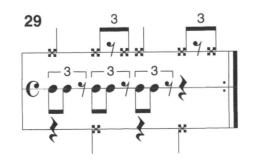

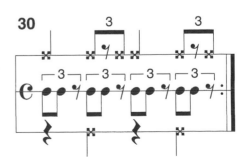

31

RC
BD
HH

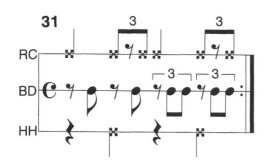

32

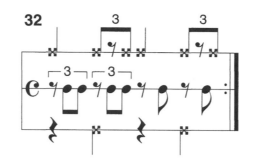

33

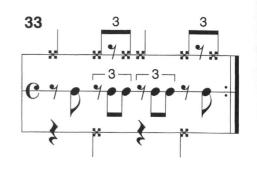

34

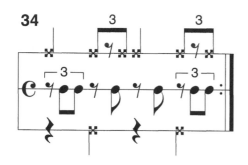

35

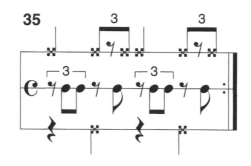

36

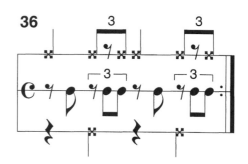

37

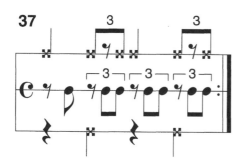

38

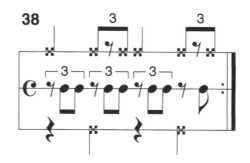

39

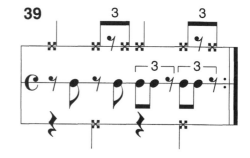

40

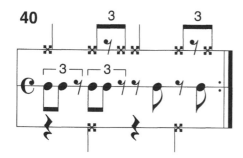

41

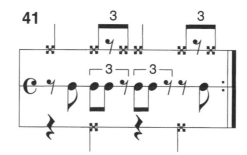

42

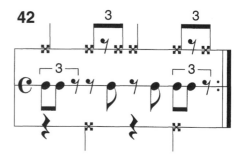

43

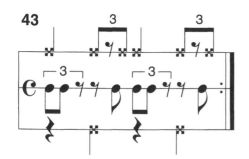

44

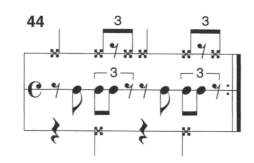

45

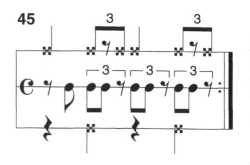

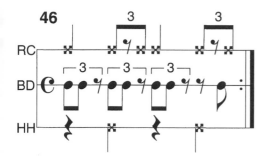

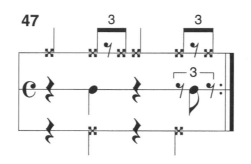

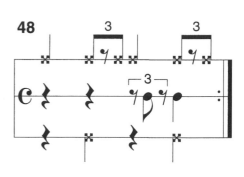

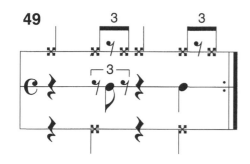

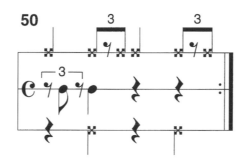

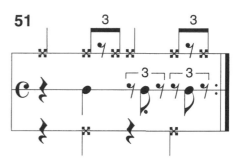

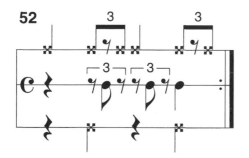

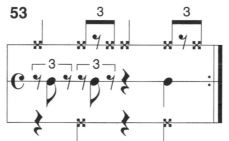

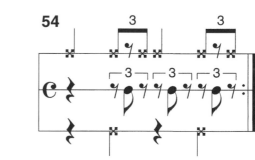

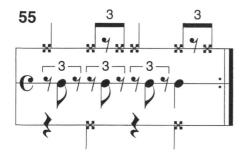

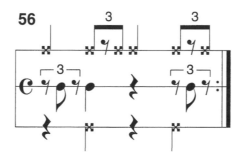

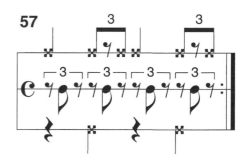

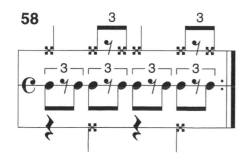

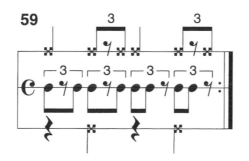

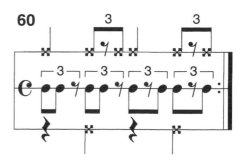

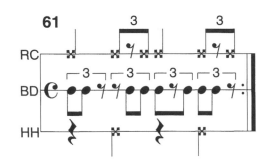

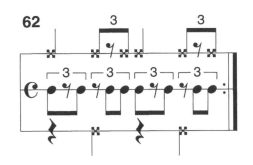

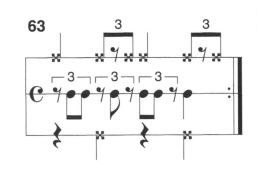

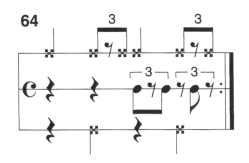

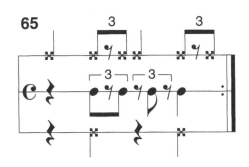

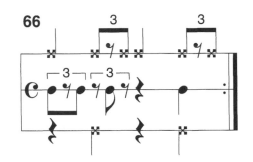

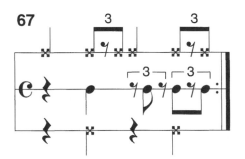

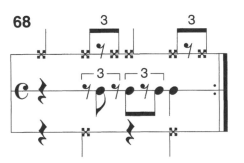

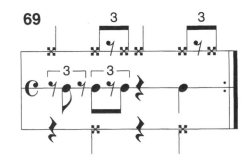

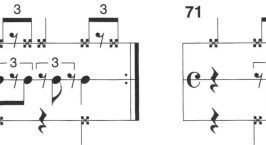

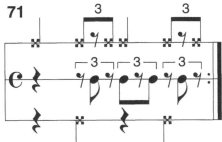

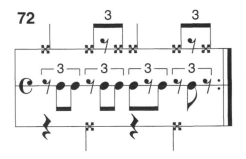

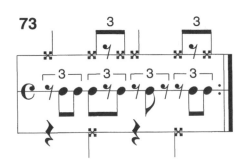

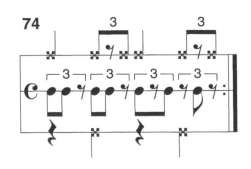

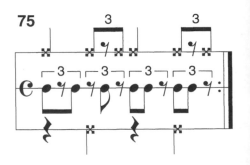

SUMMARY EXERCISE 21

SUMMARY EXERCISE 22

Note: After you've mastered Section II, there are three other ways you can practice the same material. **1)** Play all of the one-bar and Summary Exercises in *unison* (snare and bass drum together). **2)** Play *one line* of each Summary Exercise on the bass drum, then the next line on the snare drum, alternating back and forth. **3)** Play *one bar* of each Summary Exercise on the bass drum, then the next bar on the snare drum, alternating back and forth.

SECTION III: SNARE DRUM & BASS DRUM INDEPENDENCE
PART 1: QUARTER-NOTE PATTERNS

Assuming you've become proficient with the previous two sections of this book, you can now begin to work on *combining* snare drum and bass drum independence patterns. As with prior sections, practice each exercise slowly and methodically, and do not move on to the next exercise until the previous one has been mastered. We begin here with basic quarter-note snare and bass drum combination exercises.

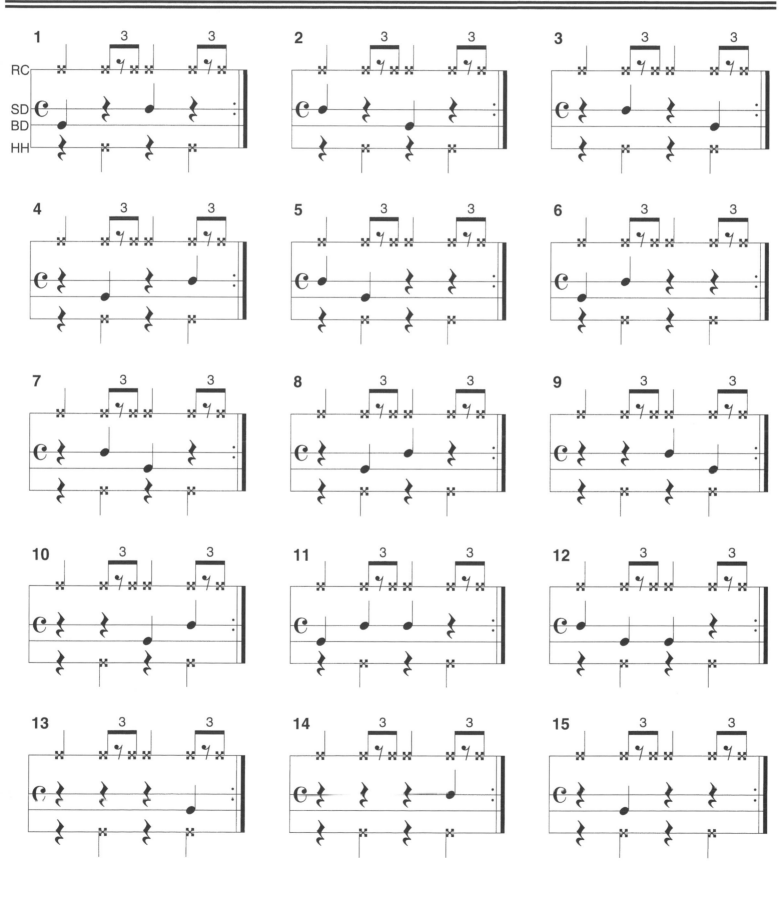

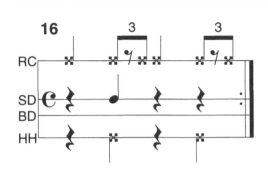

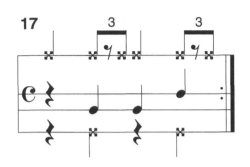

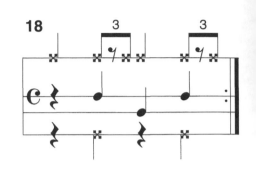

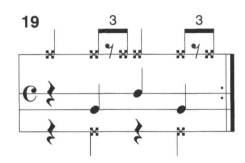

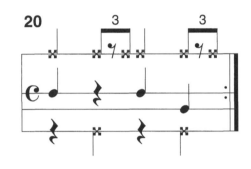

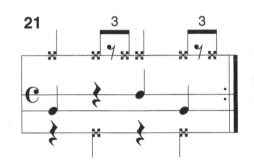

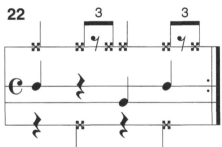

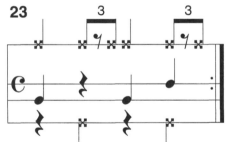

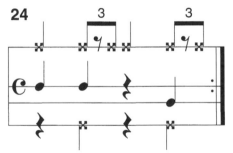

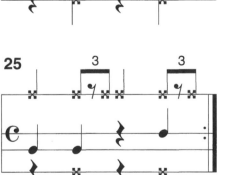

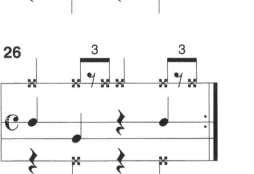

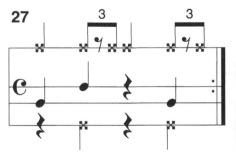

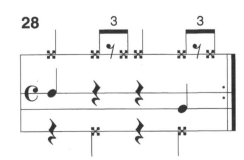

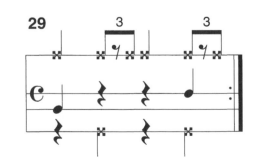

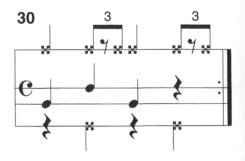

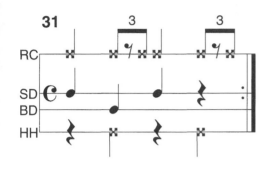

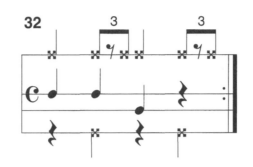

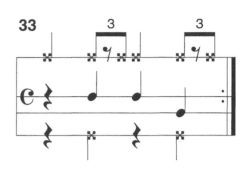

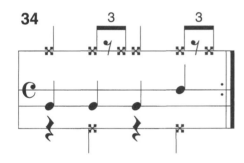

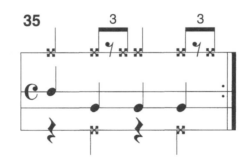

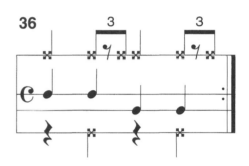

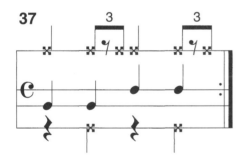

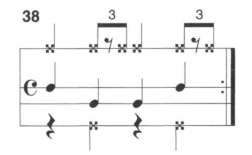

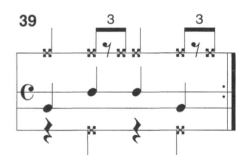

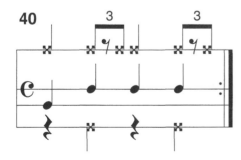

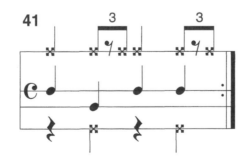

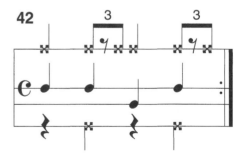

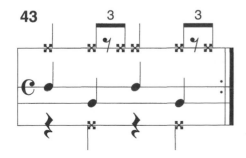

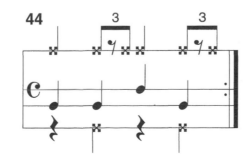

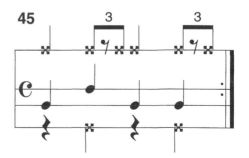

SUMMARY EXERCISE 23

SUMMARY EXERCISE 24

PART 2: 8TH-NOTE PATTERNS

The following twenty-three pages of material use snare drum and bass drum 8th-note combinations. Again, it's essential to phrase all 8th notes with a jazz conception. The one-bar exercises that follow begin simply and become more difficult as you progress through the material, so take your time.

By this point, both the ride cymbal and hi-hat parts should be functioning on their own with little or no conscious thought involved. If you're still having problems, go back and review the material in Sections I and II.

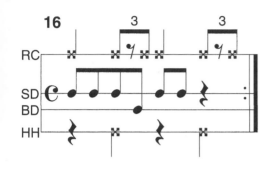

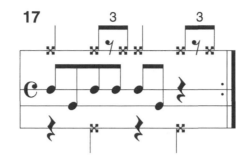

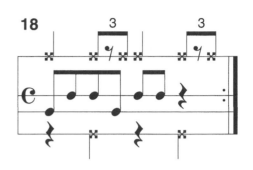

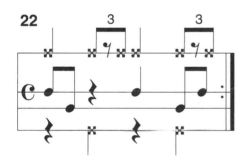

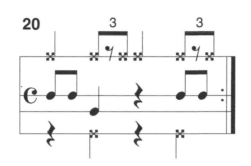

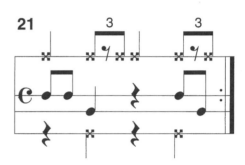

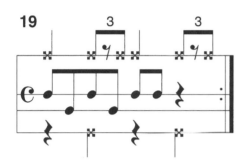

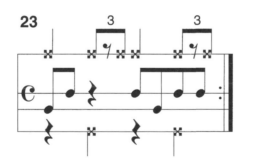

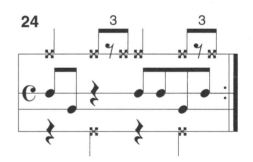

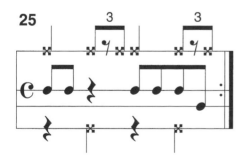

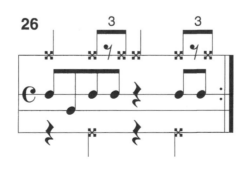

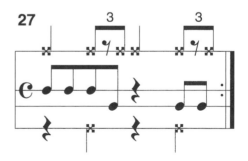

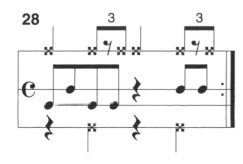

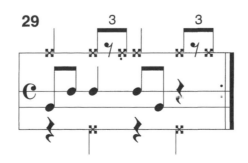

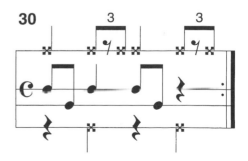

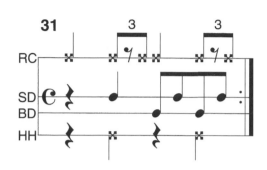
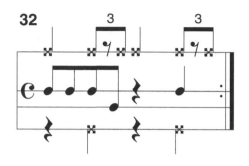
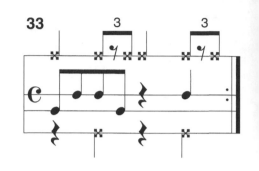
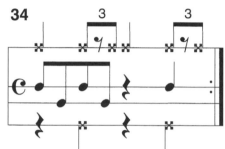
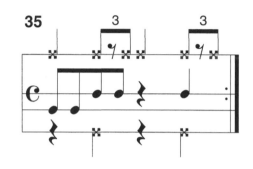
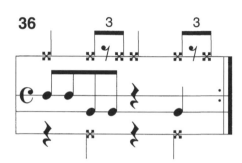

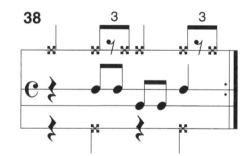
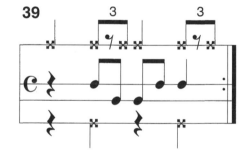
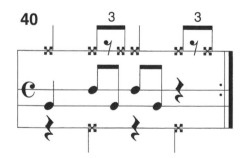
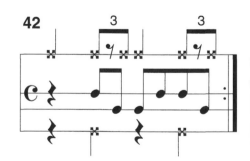
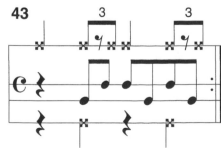
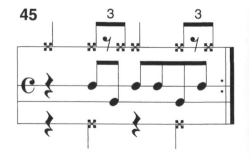

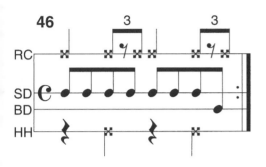

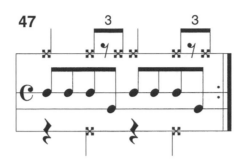

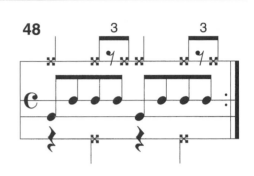

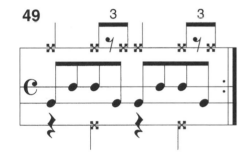

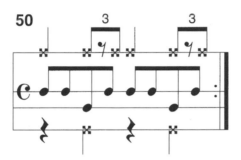

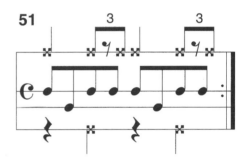

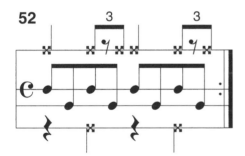

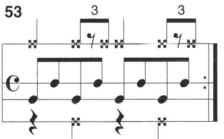

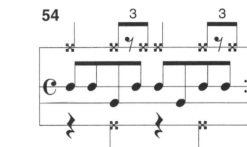

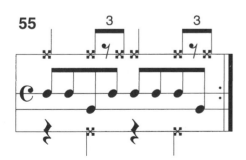

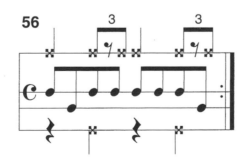

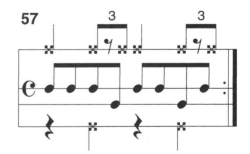

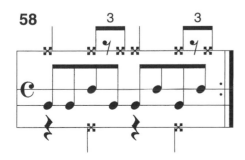

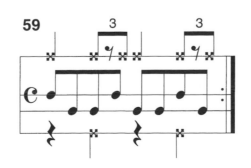

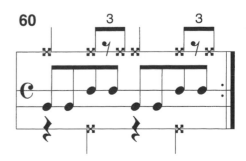

61

RC
SD
BD
HH

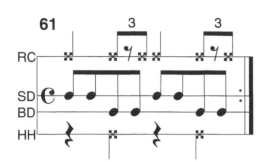

62

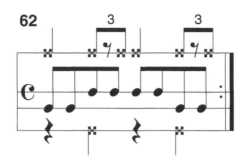

63

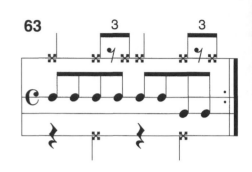

64

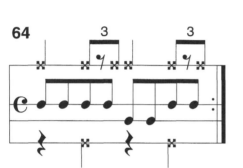

65

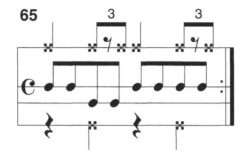

66

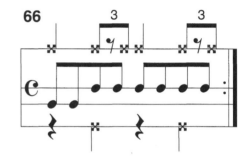

67

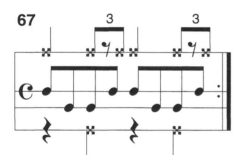

68

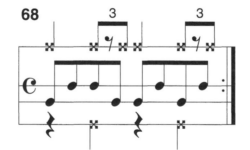

69

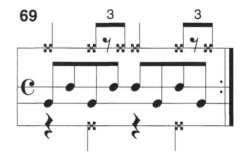

70

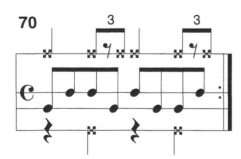

71

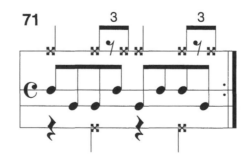

72

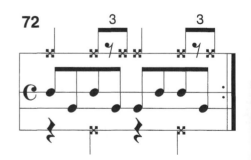

73

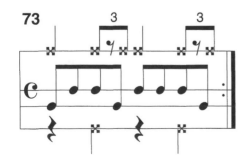

74

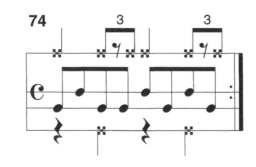

75

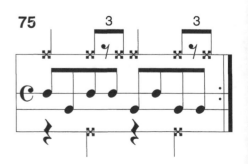

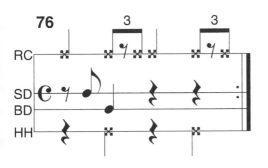
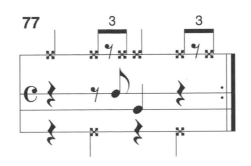
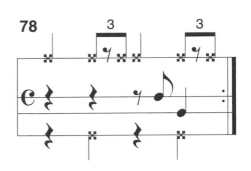

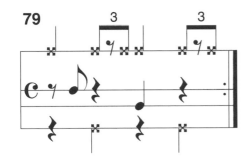
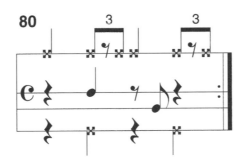
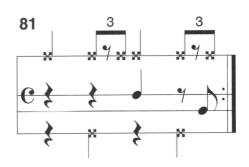

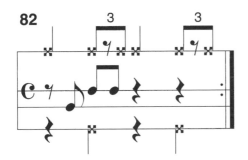
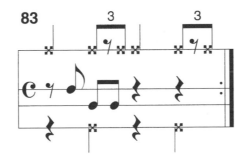
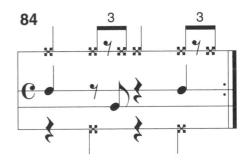

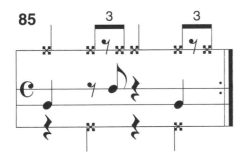
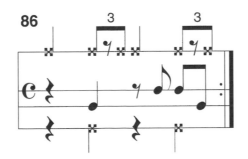
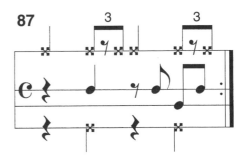

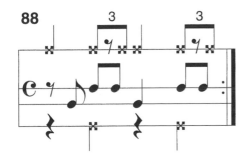
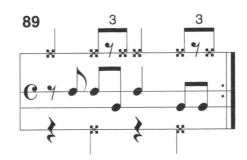
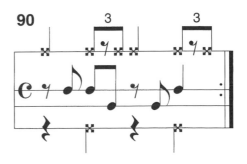

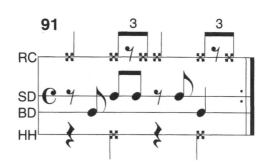

91

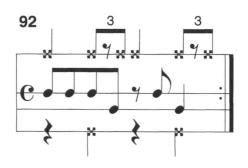

92

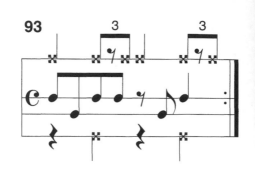

93

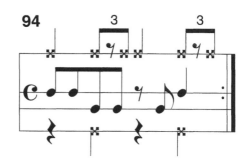

94

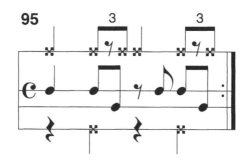

95

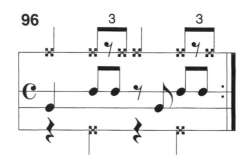

96

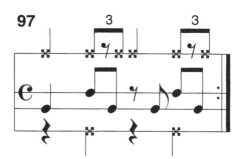

97

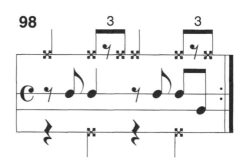

98

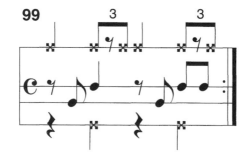

99

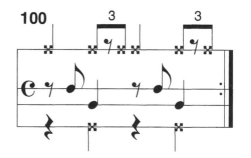

100

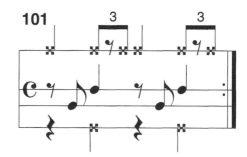

101

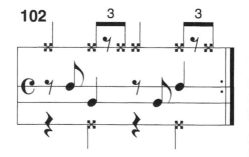

102

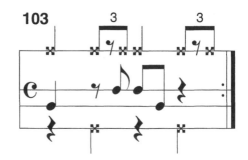

103

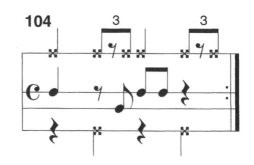

104

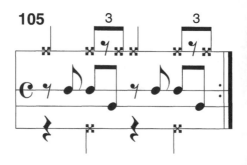

105

106
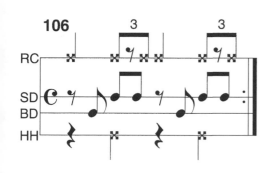

107
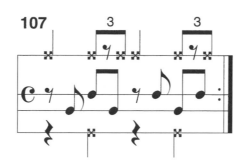

108
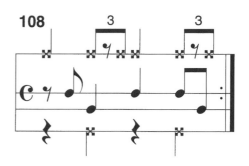

109
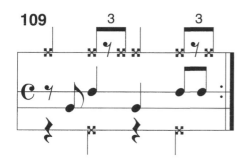

110
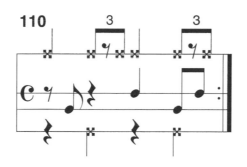

111
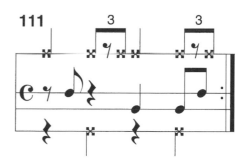

112
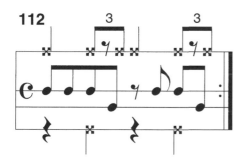

113
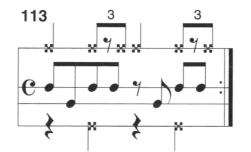

114
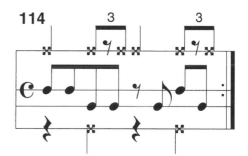

115
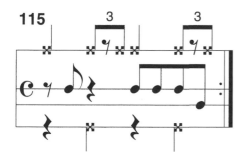

116
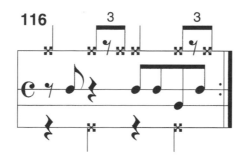

117
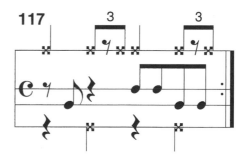

118
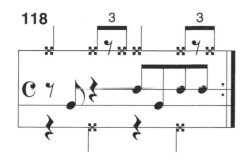

119
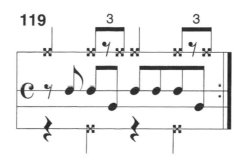

120
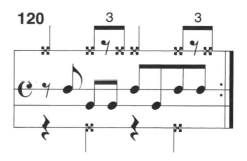

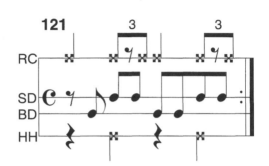
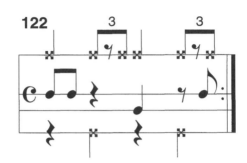
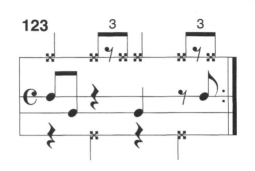

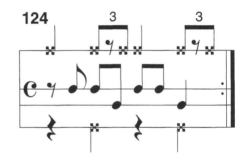
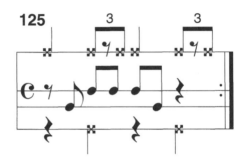
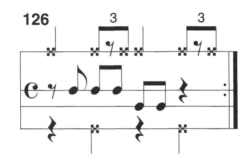

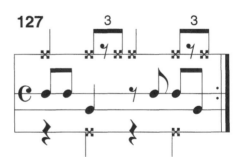
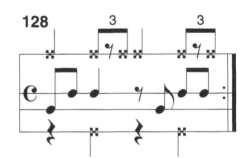
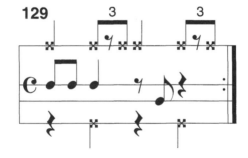

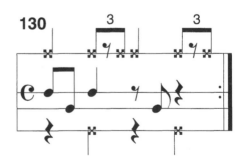
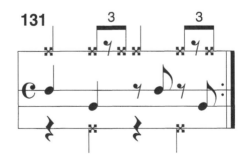
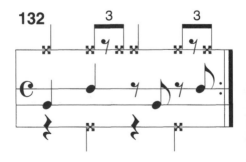

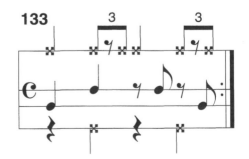
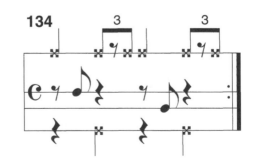
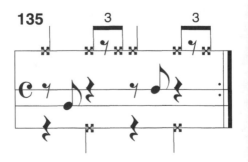

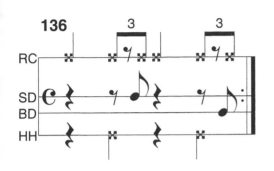

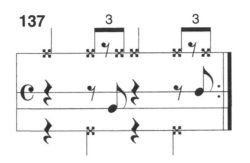

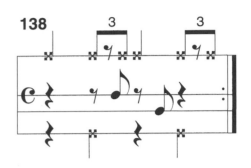

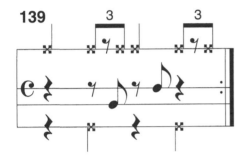

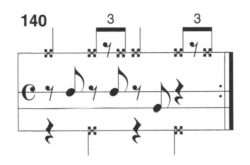

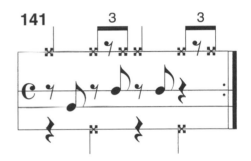

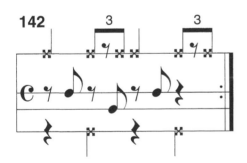

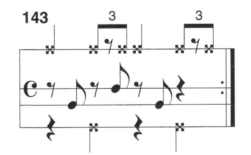

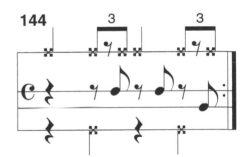

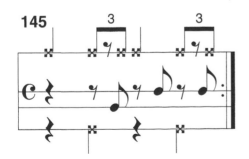

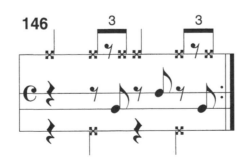

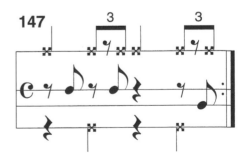

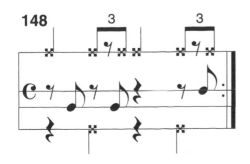

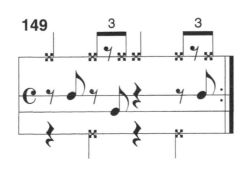

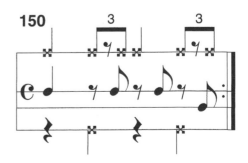

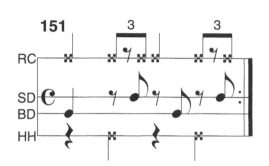

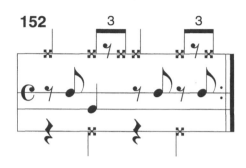

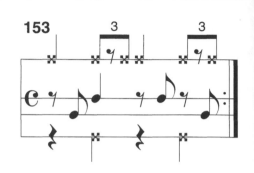

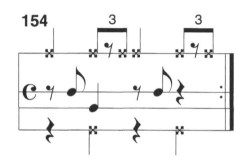

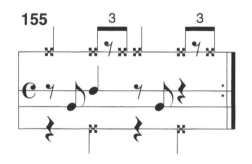

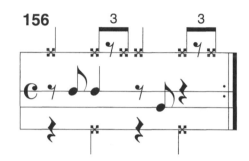

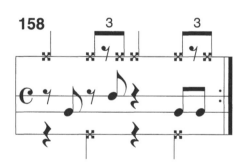

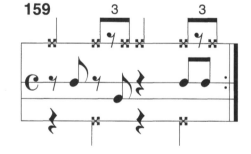

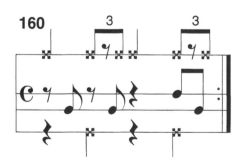

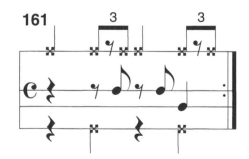

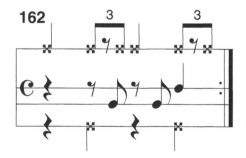

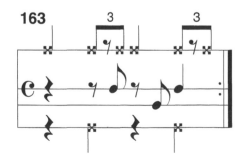

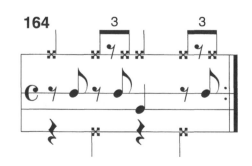

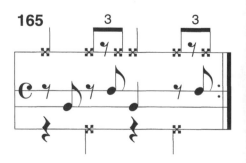

166
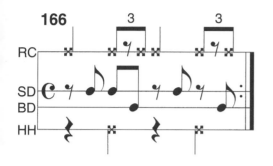

167
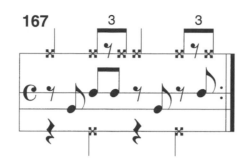

168
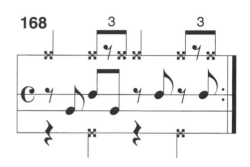

169
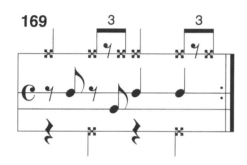

170
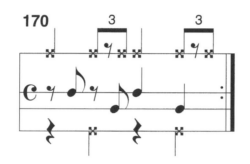

171
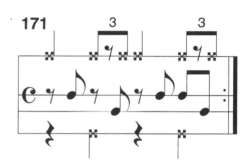

172
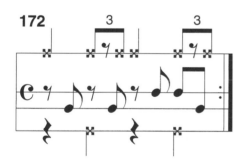

173
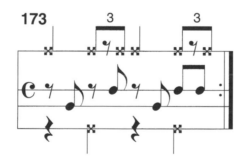

174
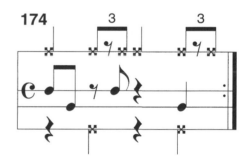

175
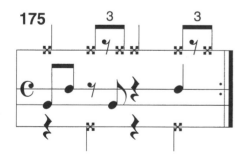

176
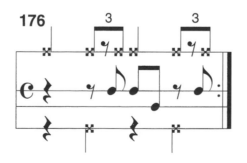

177
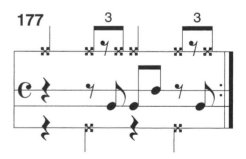

178
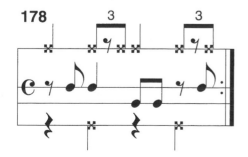

179
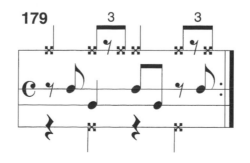

180
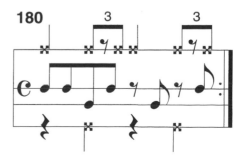

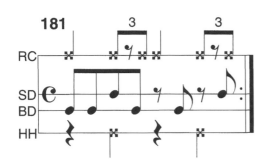
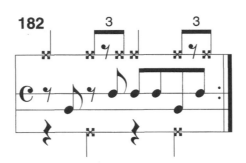
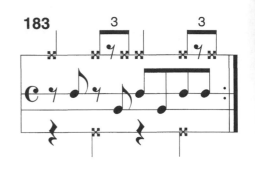
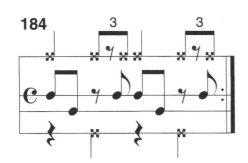
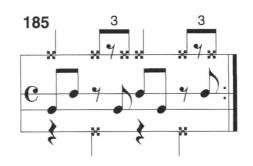
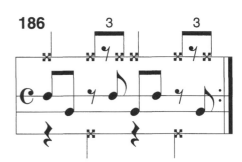
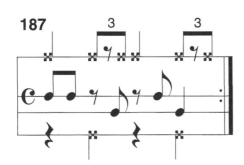
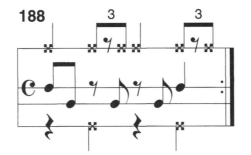
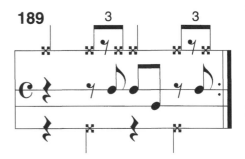
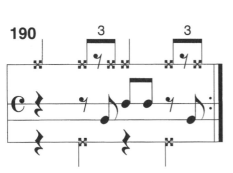
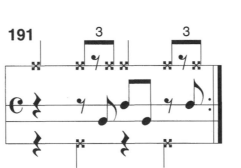
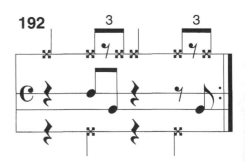
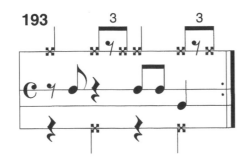
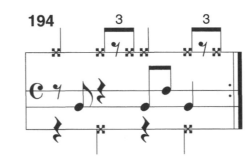
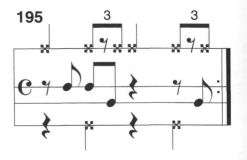

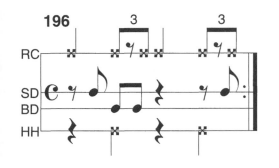

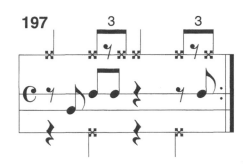

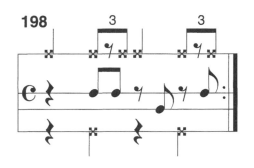

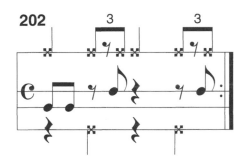

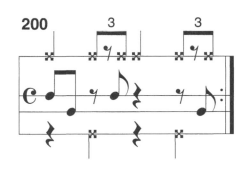

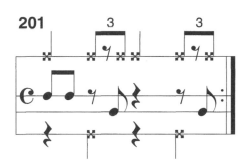

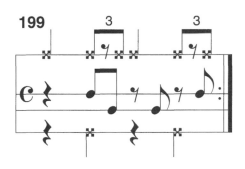

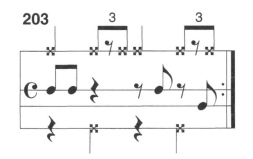

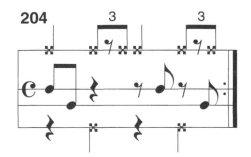

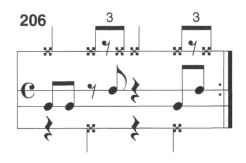

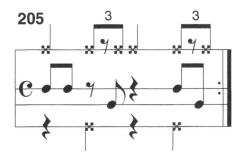

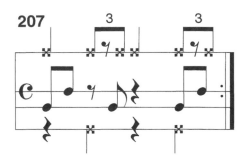

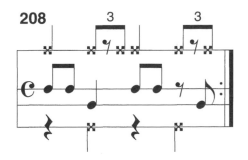

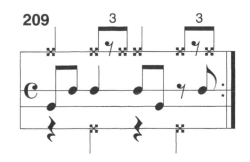

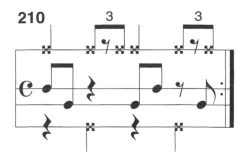

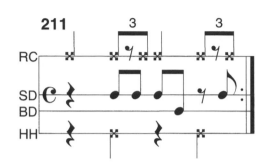

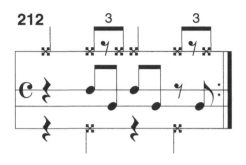

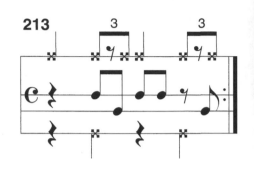

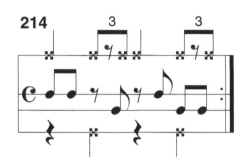

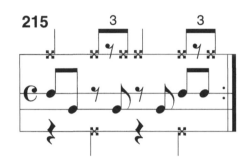

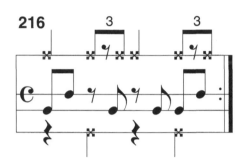

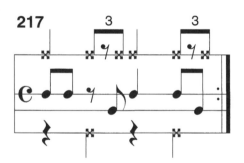

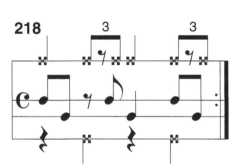

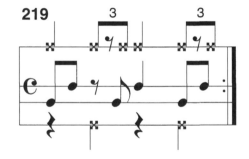

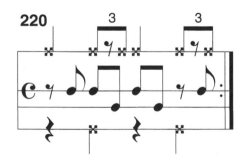

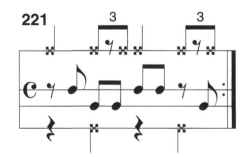

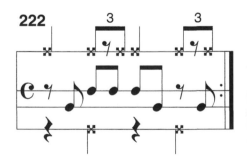

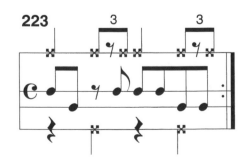

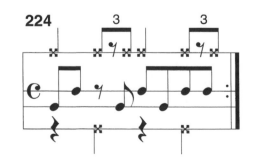

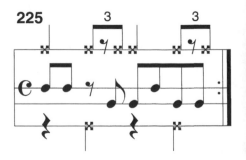

SUMMARY EXERCISE 25

SUMMARY EXERCISE 26

SUMMARY EXERCISE 27

SUMMARY EXERCISE 28

SUMMARY EXERCISE 29

SUMMARY EXERCISE 30

SUMMARY EXERCISE 31

SUMMARY EXERCISE 32

PART 3: SYNCOPATED PATTERNS

Ensemble cues, or "kicks," are often notated on big band drum charts. Fluency with the syncopated patterns that follow will help you accurately and spontaneously orchestrate figures between the snare drum and bass drum for a more musical interpretation of these arrangements. As in the previous two sections, a slight emphasis on all the quarter notes and any 8th note that is not immediately followed by another note will produce a more natural jazz groove.

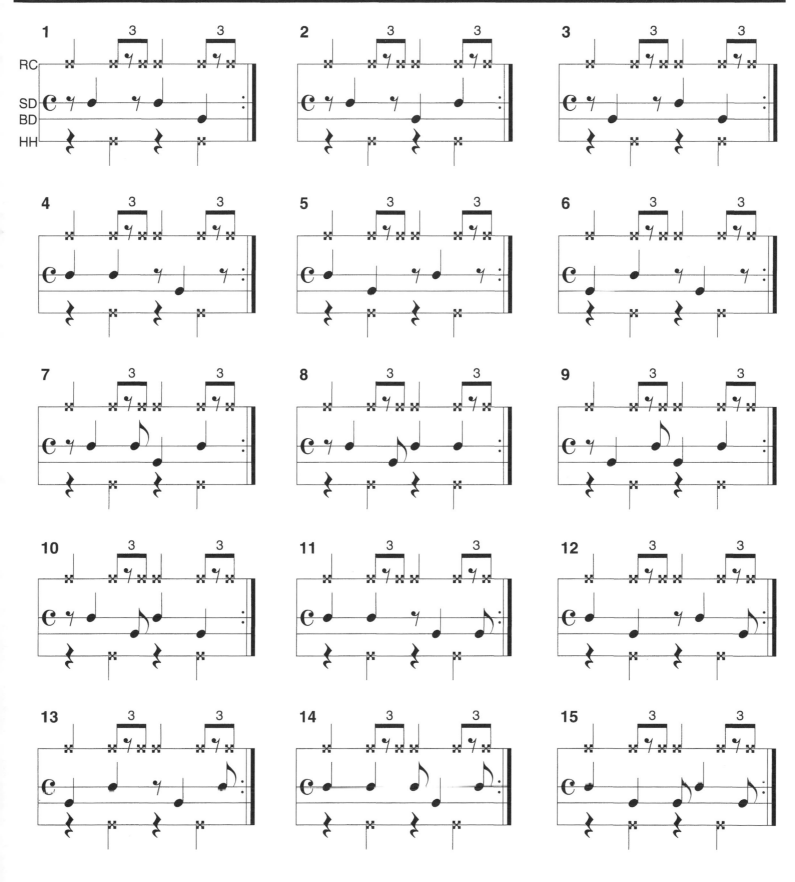

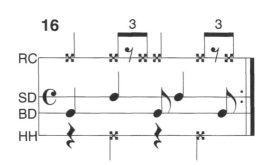

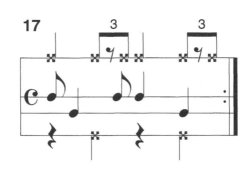

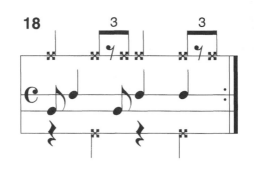

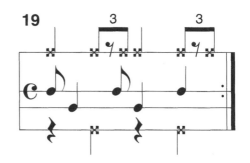

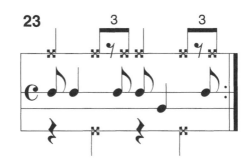

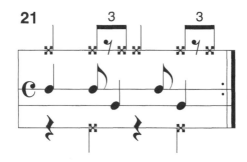

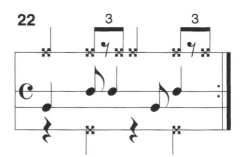

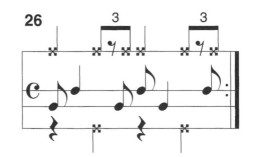

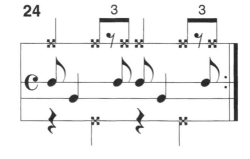

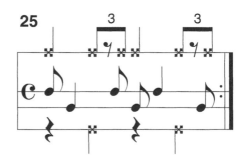

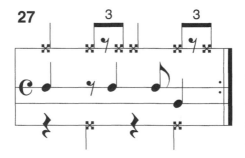

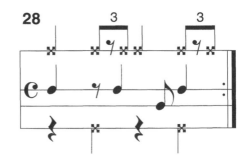

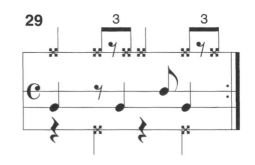

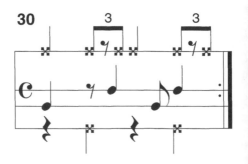

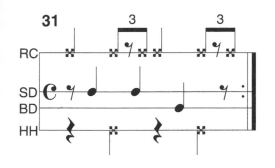

31

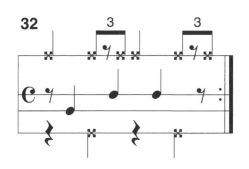

32

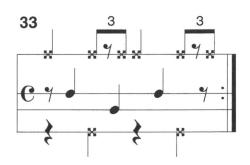

33

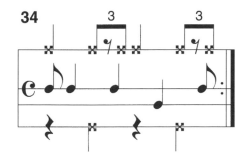

34

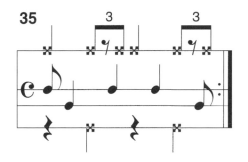

35

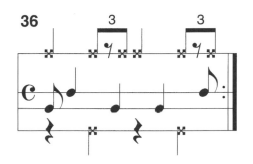

36

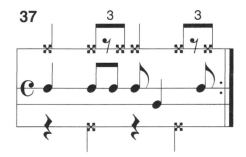

37

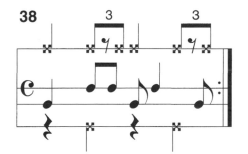

38

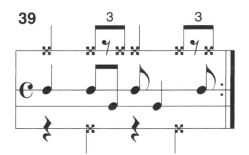

39

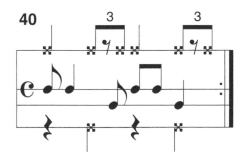

40

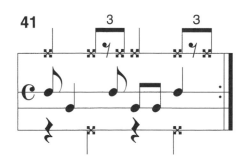

41

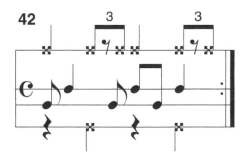

42

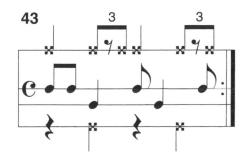

43

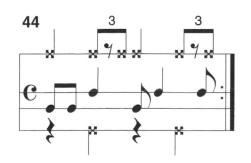

44

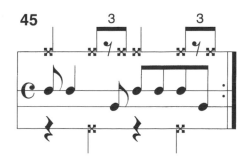

45

91

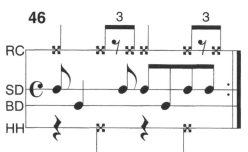
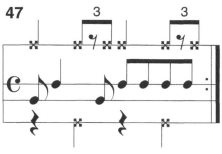
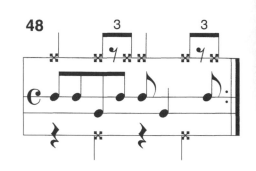

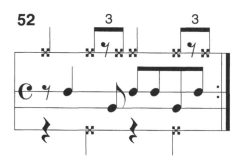
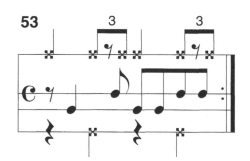
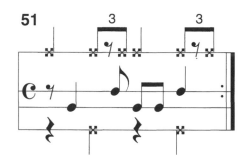

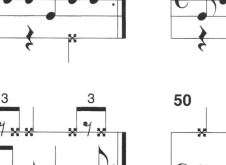
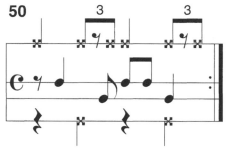
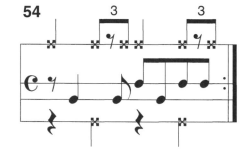

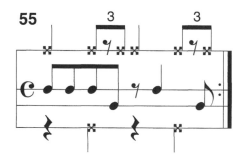
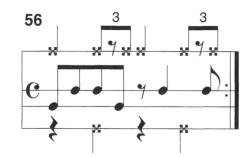
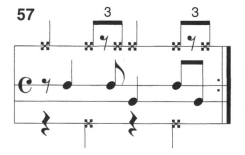

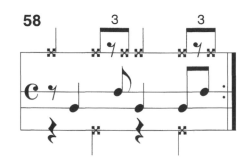
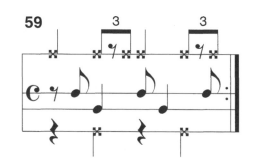
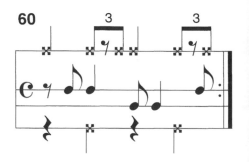

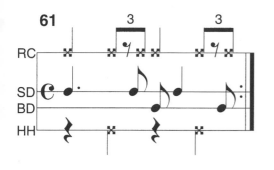

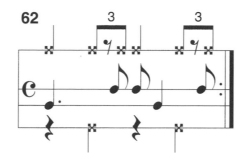

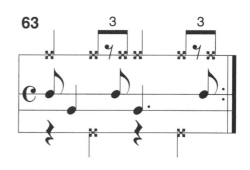

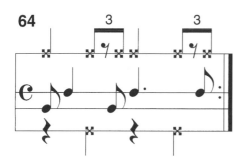

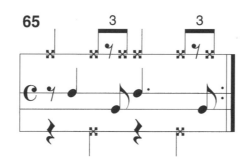

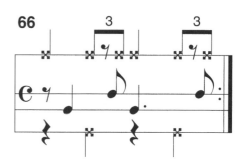

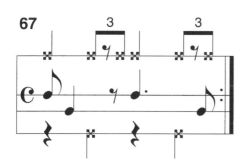

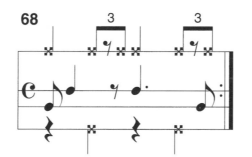

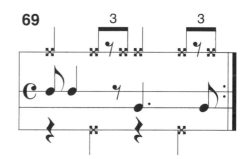

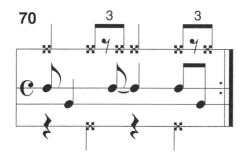

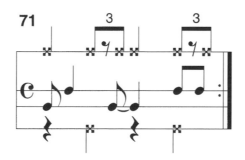

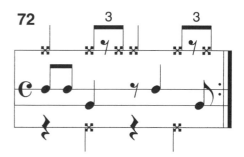

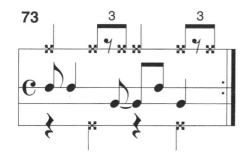

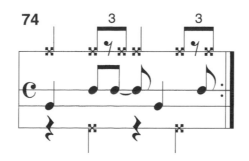

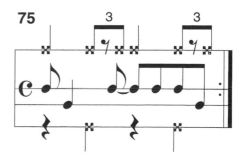

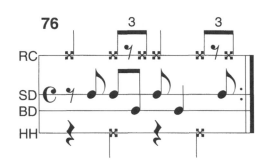

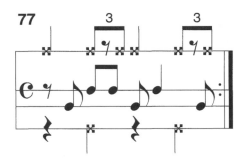

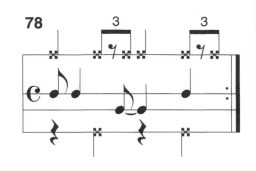

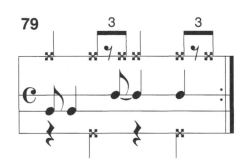

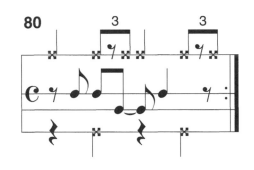

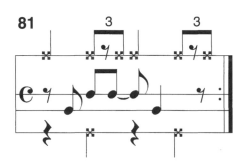

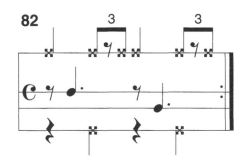

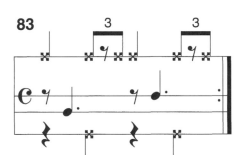

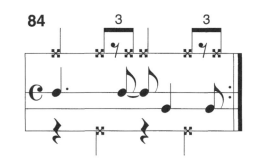

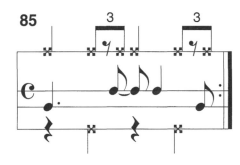

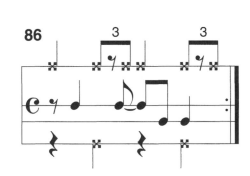

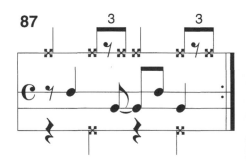

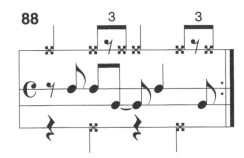

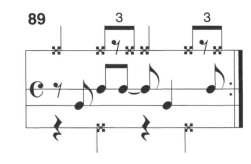

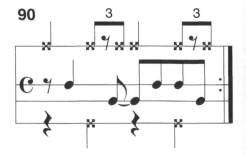

94

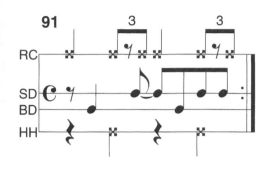

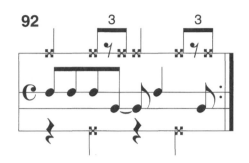

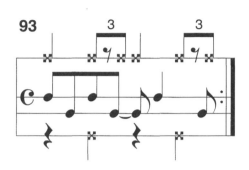

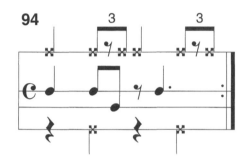

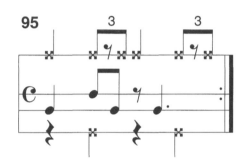

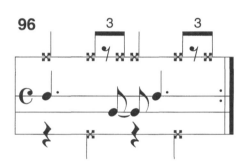

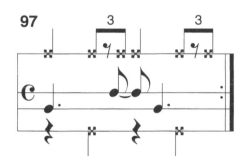

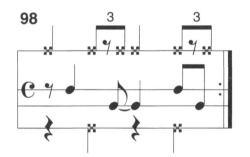

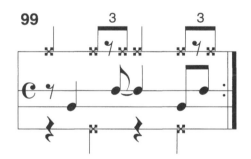

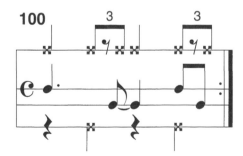

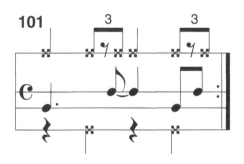

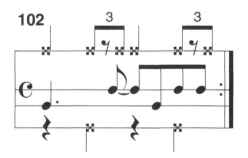

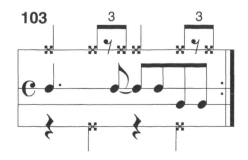

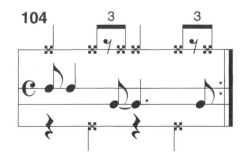

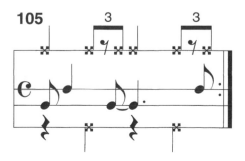

SUMMARY EXERCISE 33

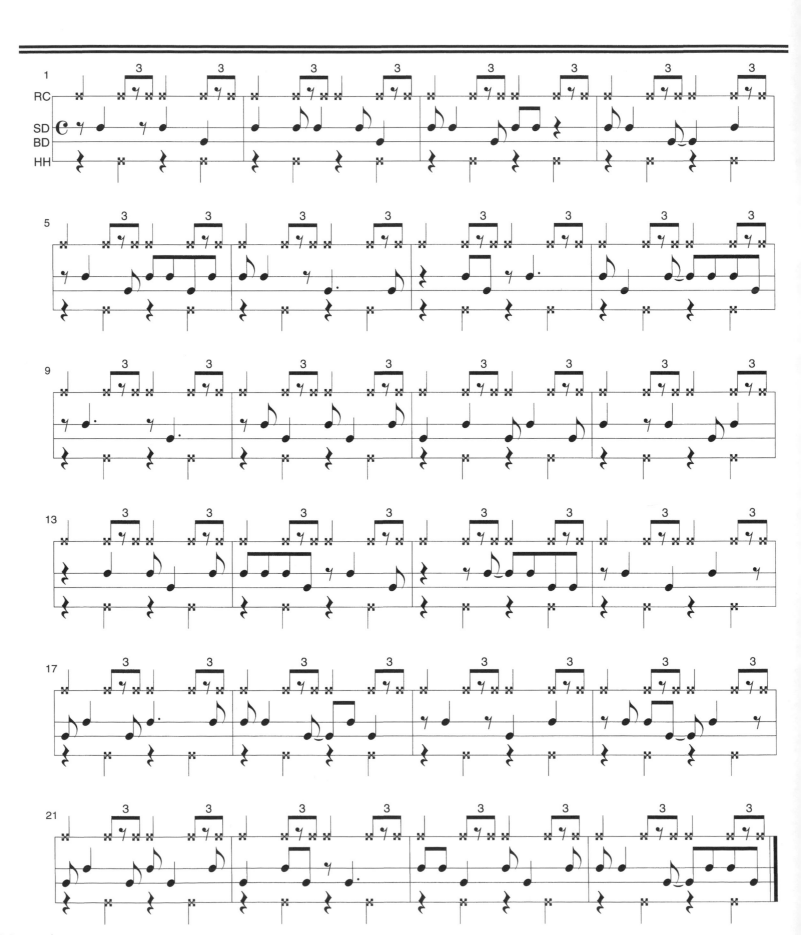

SUMMARY EXERCISE 34

SUMMARY EXERCISE 35

SUMMARY EXERCISE 36

PART 4: TRIPLET PATTERNS

The one-bar triplet independence exercises in this section have the bass drum falling on various notes of the triplet.
We begin here with the bass drum on the downbeats (exercises 1-11), and progress to the "a" (exercises 12-22).

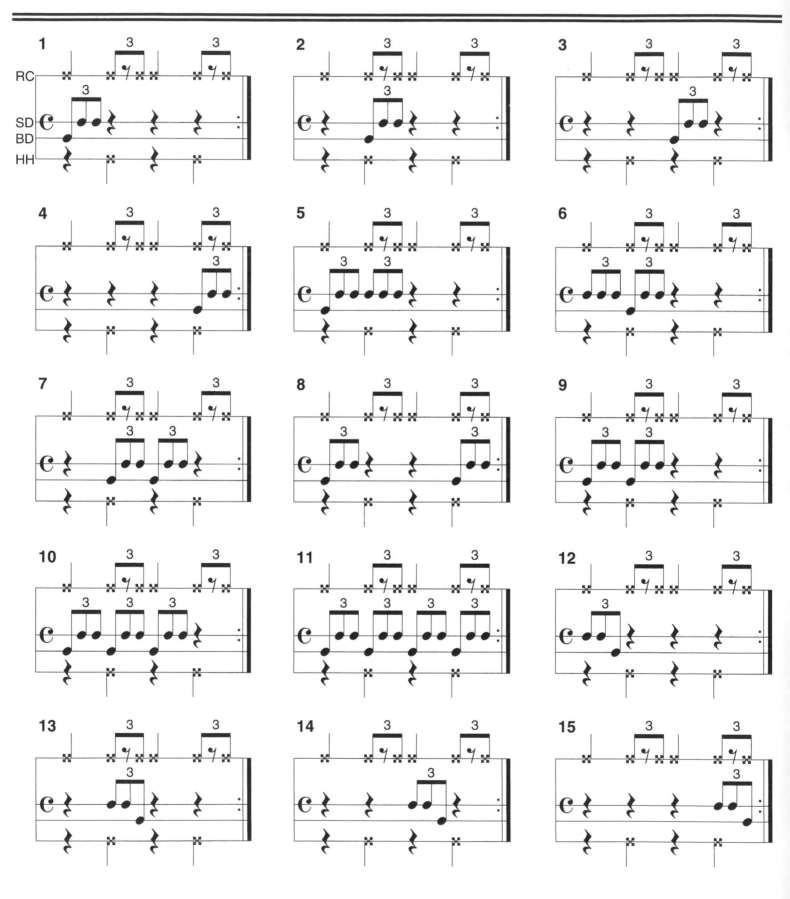

Accurately placing the bass drum on the middle note of the triplet (beginning with 23) can be tricky. Take sufficient time with these patterns.

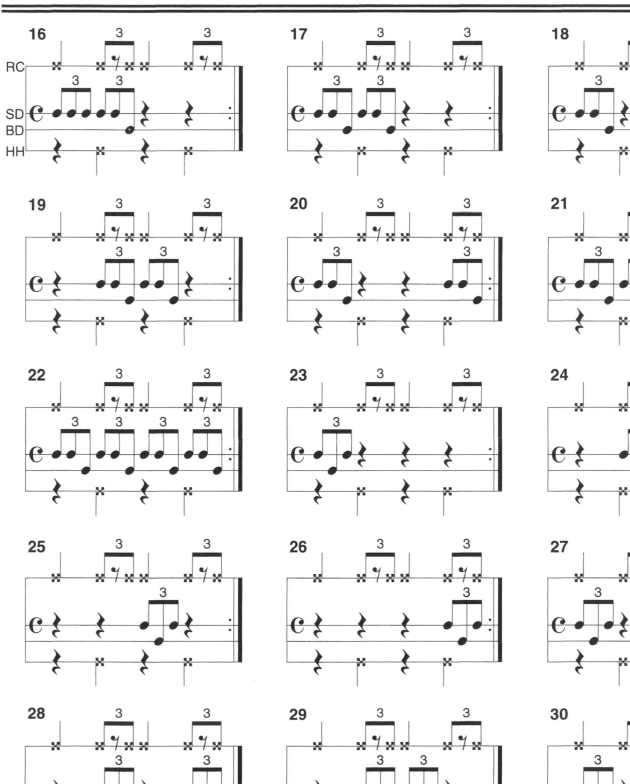

An interesting effect is created in exercise 34 when the bass drum falls on the downbeat and the "a," and the snare drum occurs on the "an." Note the bass drum "shuffle" feel created in exercise 45.

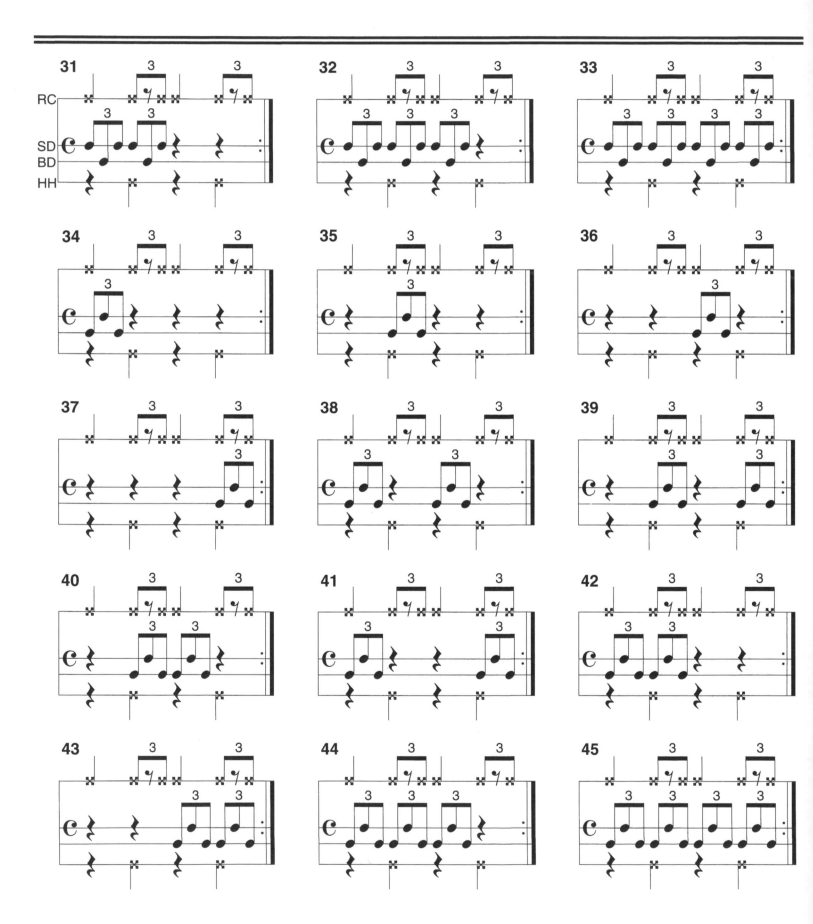

Here are some combinations of the previous triplet patterns. Maintain a steady tempo and don't rush the triplets.

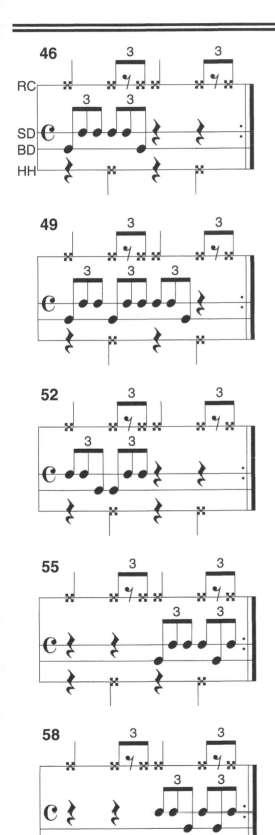
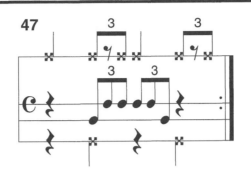
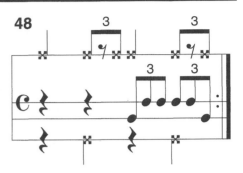
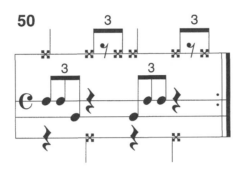
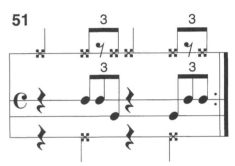
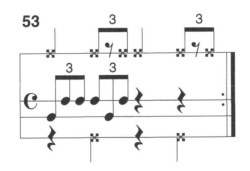
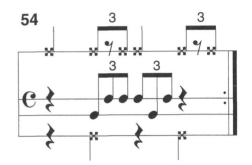
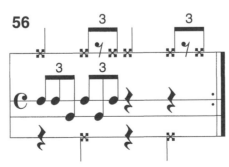
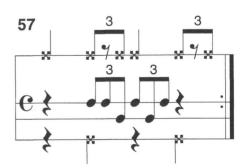
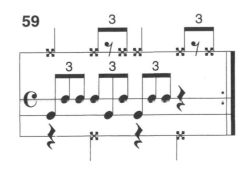
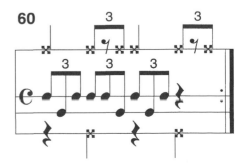

Exercises 69 through 77 can present a control challenge for the bass drum foot. Take them slowly at first.

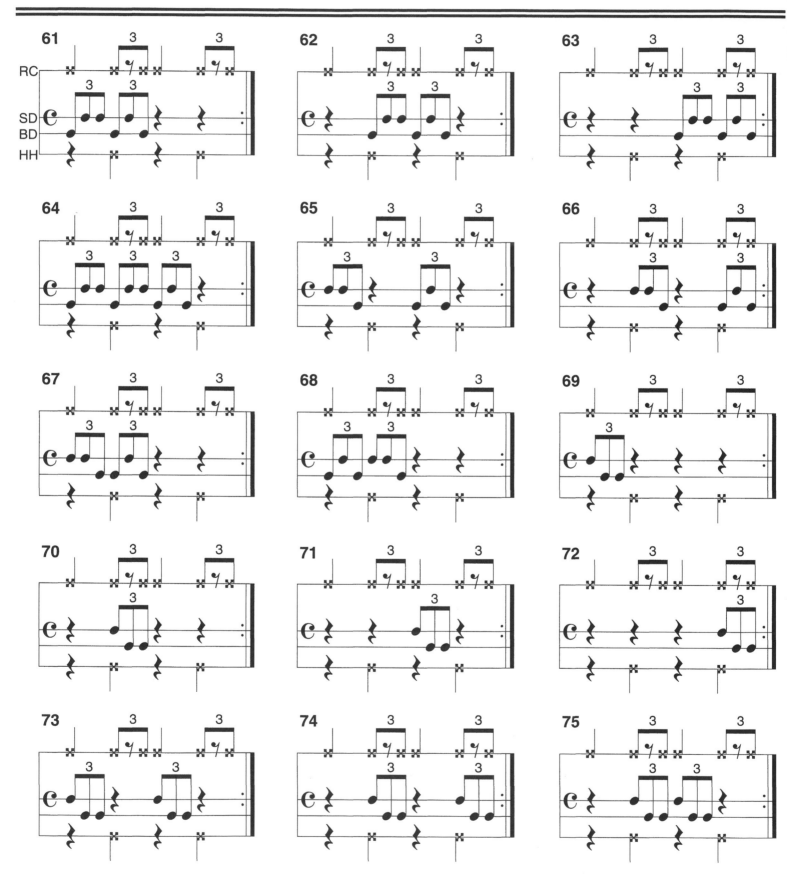

These triplet independence combinations produce some very interesting rhythmic possibilities. Practice them with a metronome.

76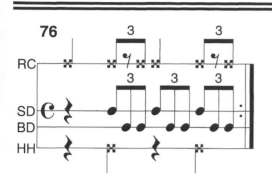

77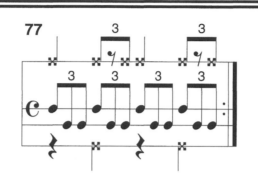

78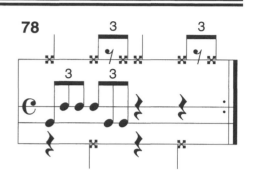

79

80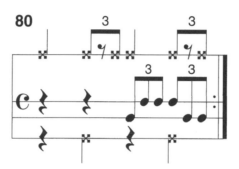

81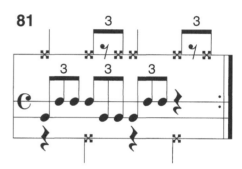

82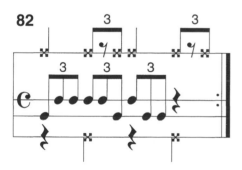

83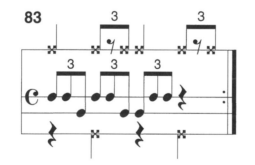

84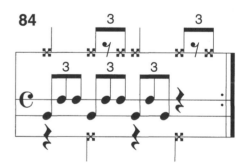

85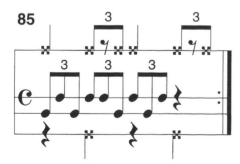

86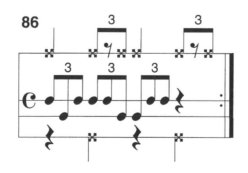

87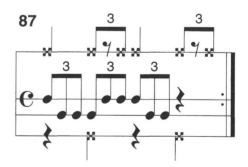

88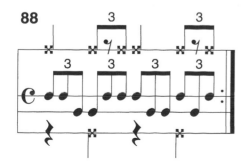

89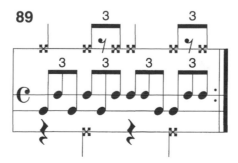

90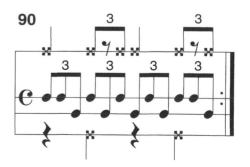

Alternating triplet partials between snare drum and bass drum can result in some dynamic polyrhythmic effects. Repeat each exercise as many times as needed until you've achieved a smooth, natural flow.

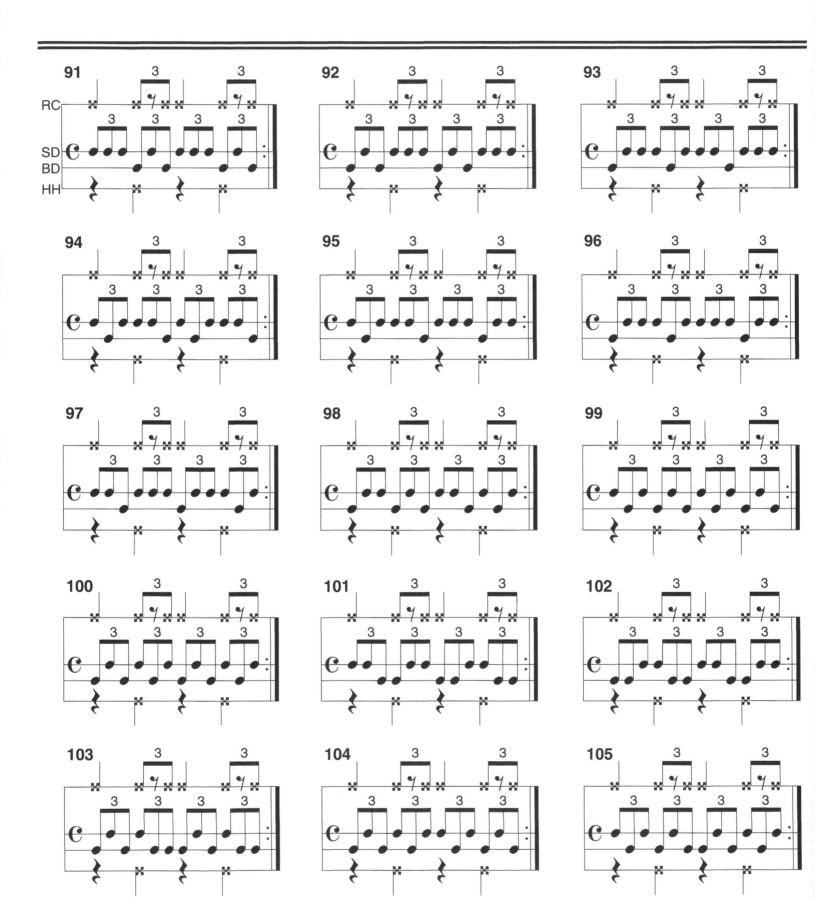

TRIPLET AND 8TH-NOTE COMBINATIONS

Be sure to maintain the "swung 8th note" concept throughout the following exercises, which use most of the triplet combinations from the previous pages.

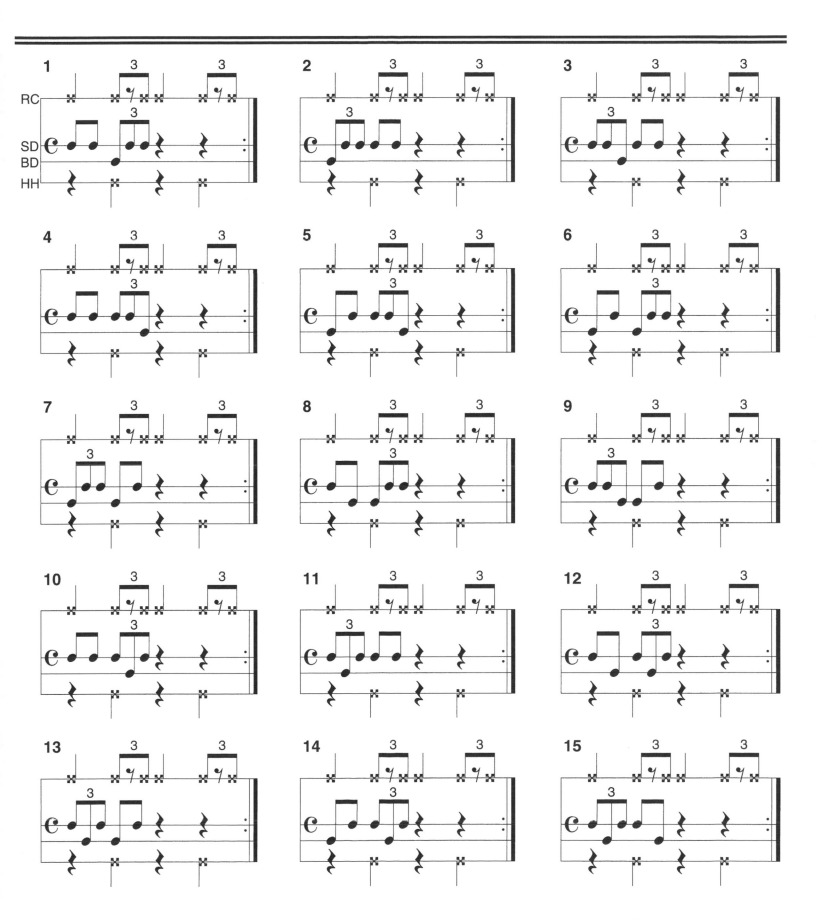

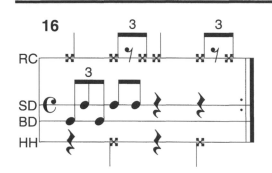

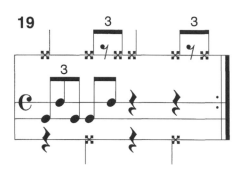

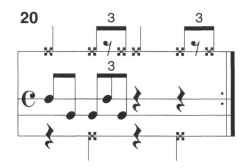

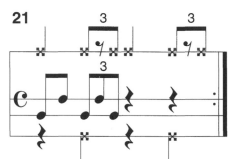

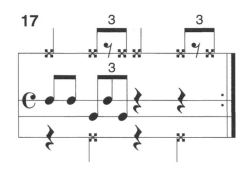

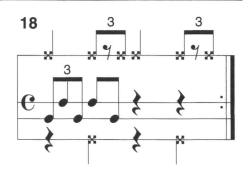

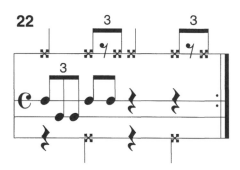

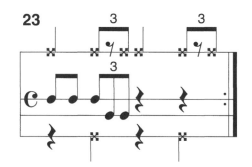

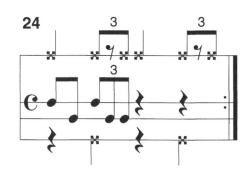

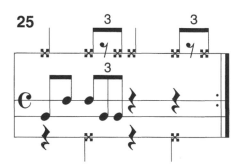

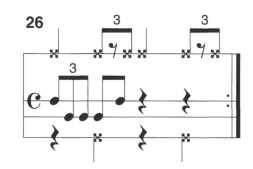

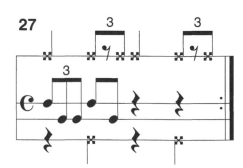

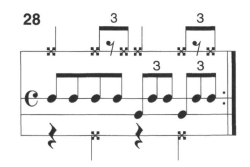

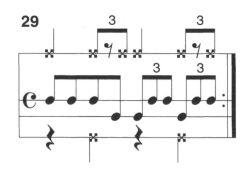

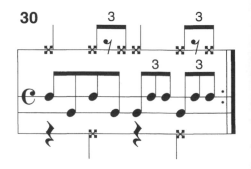

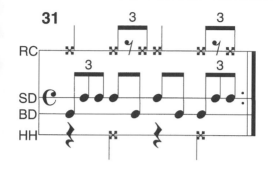

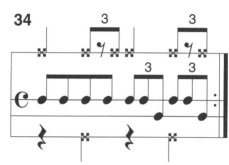

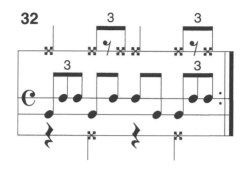

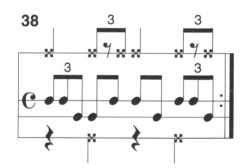

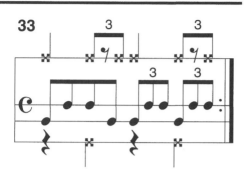

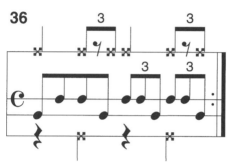

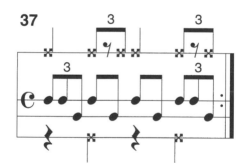

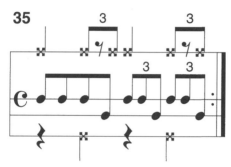

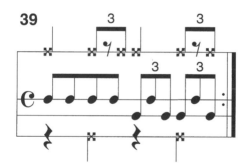

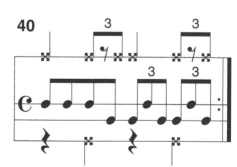

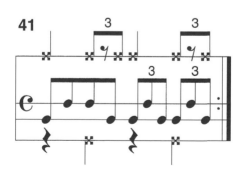

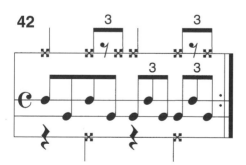

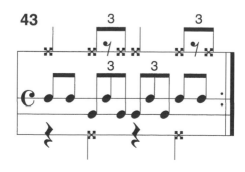

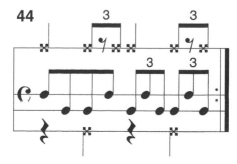

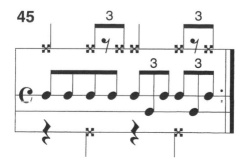

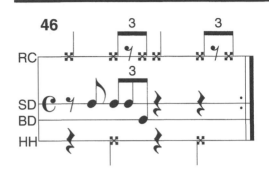
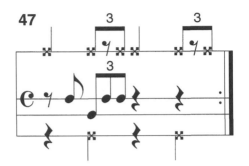
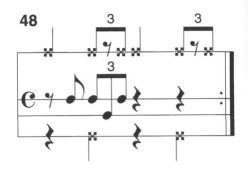

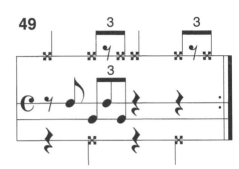
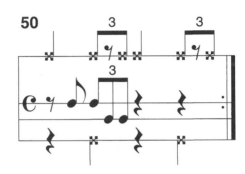
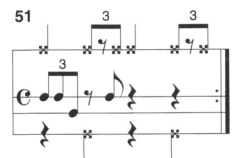

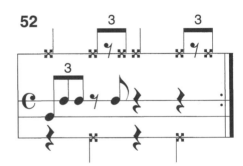
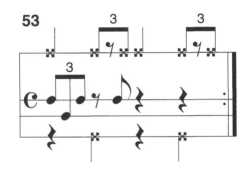
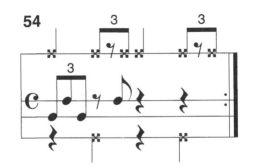

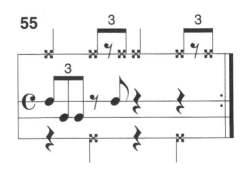
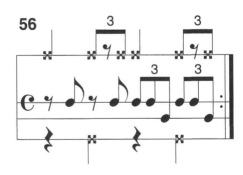
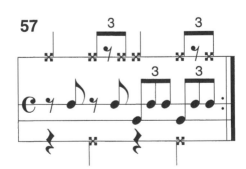

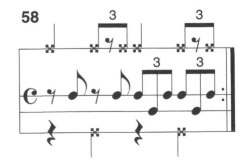
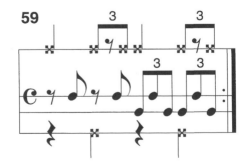
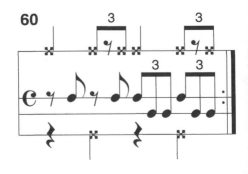

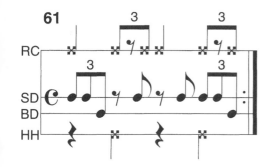
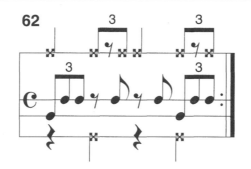
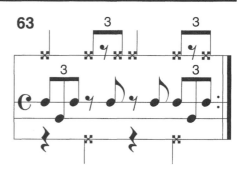

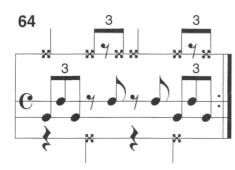
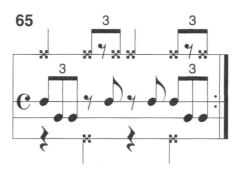
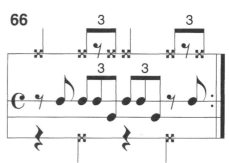

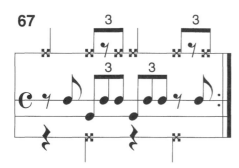
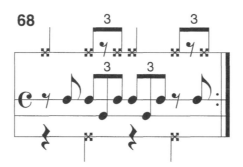
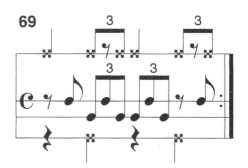

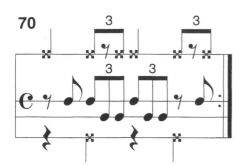
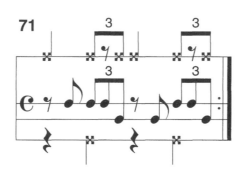
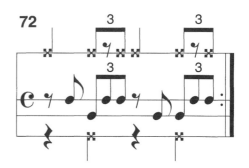

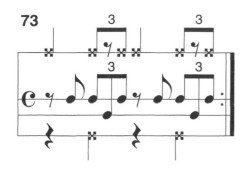
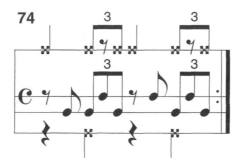
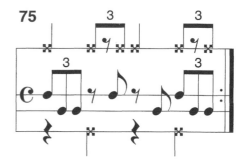

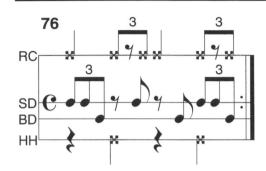

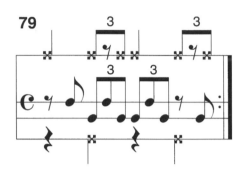

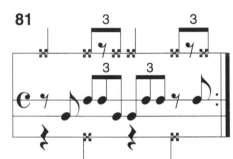

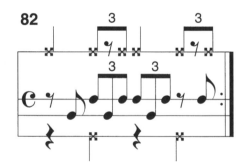

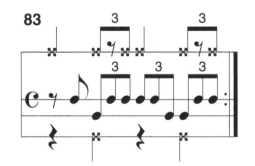

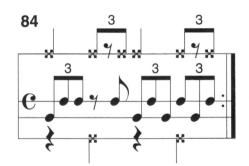

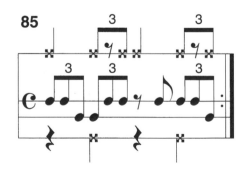

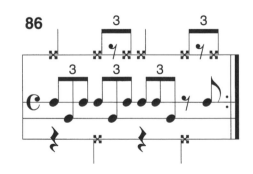

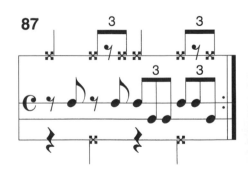

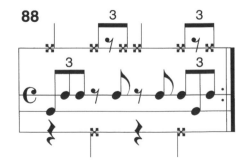

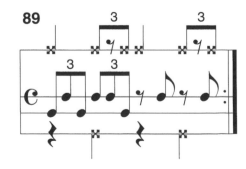

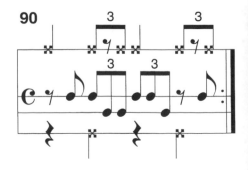

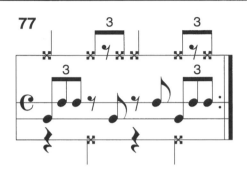

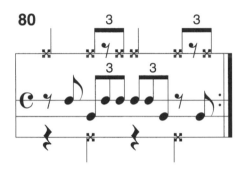

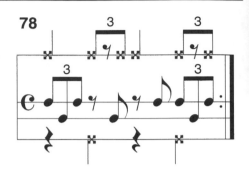

SUMMARY EXERCISE 37

SUMMARY EXERCISE 38

TRIPLET PARTIALS

Triplet partials alternating between snare drum and bass drum can present a real coordination challenge. We begin here with the bass drum on the third partial of the triplet, and then on the second partial starting with exercise 12.

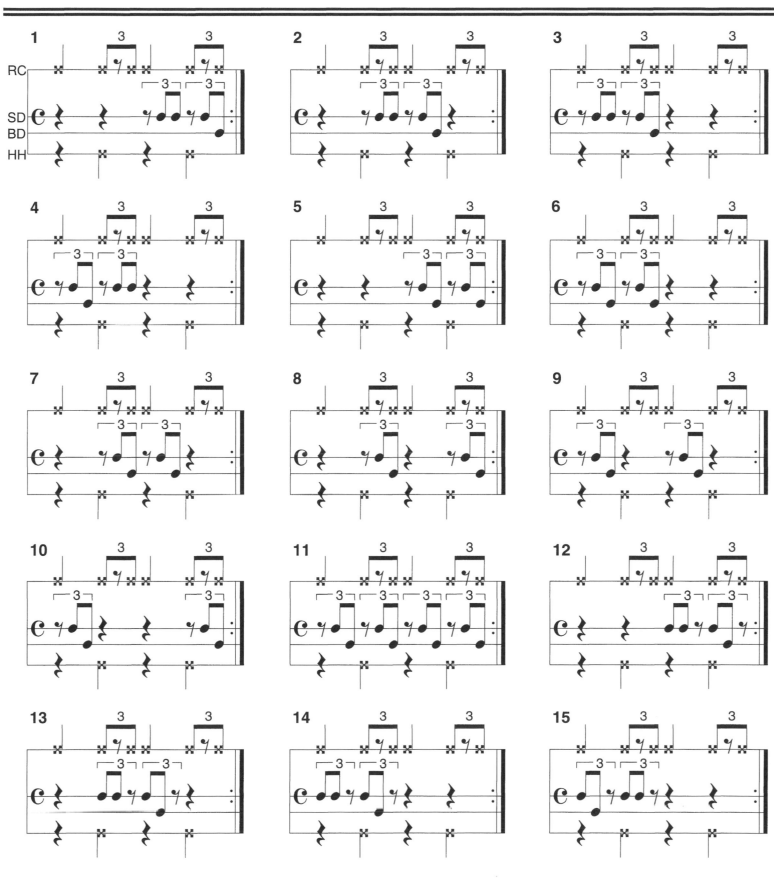

Take the exercises on this page very slowly at first, and do not move on to the next exercise until the previous one has been mastered. Note exercises 23-36, where both of the previously covered triplet partial figures occur in the same measure.

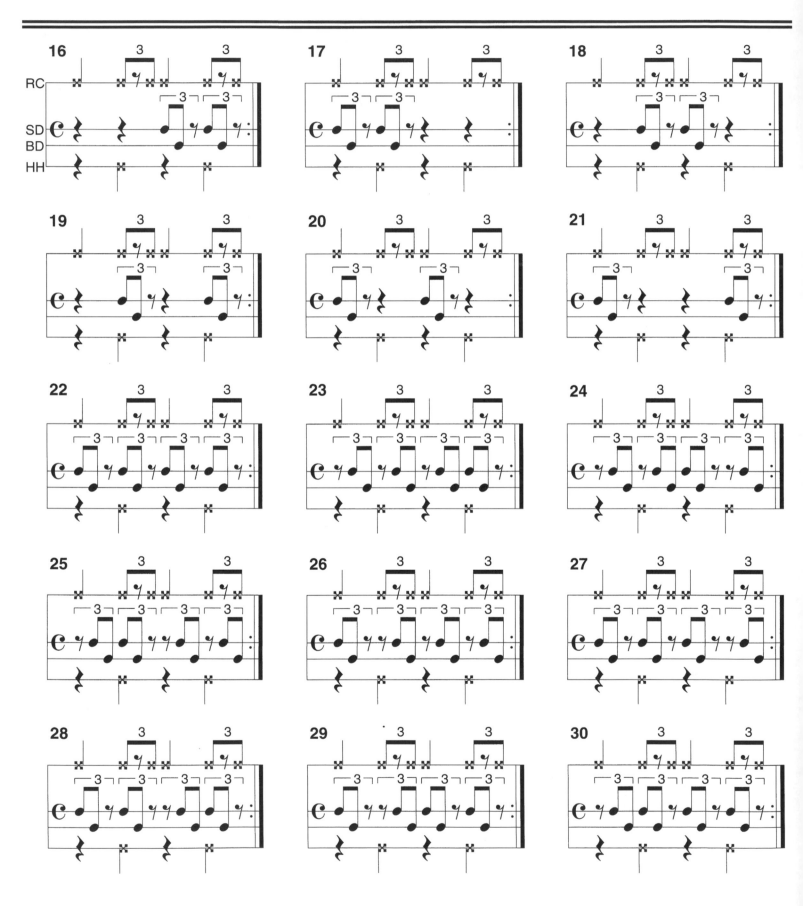

Playing the third partial of the triplet (exercises 37-45) will sound the same as playing an 8th note with a jazz conception. Strive for a swinging, solid time feel.

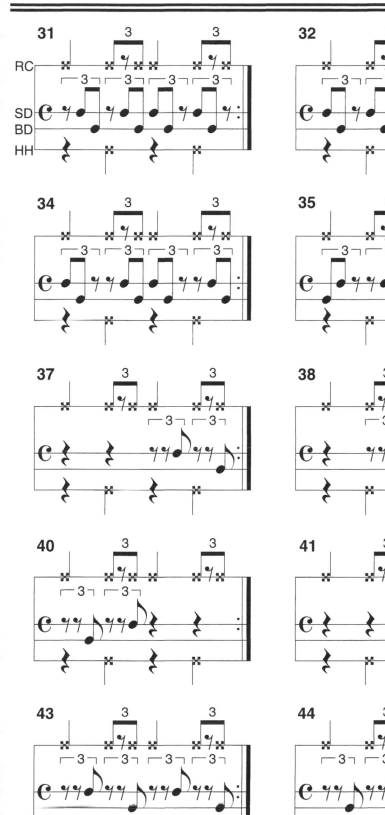
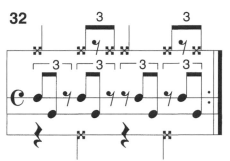
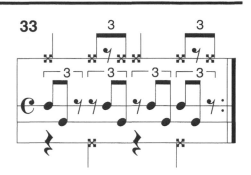
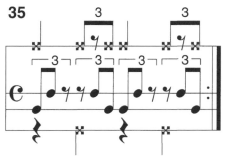
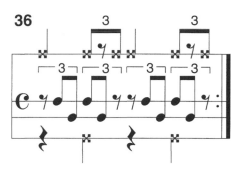
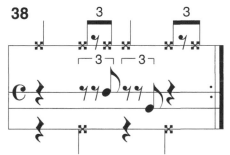
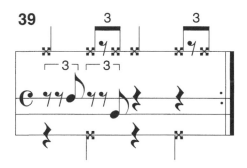
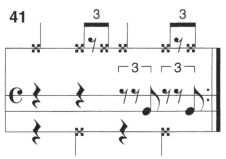
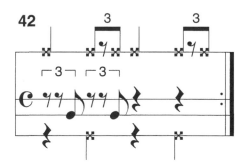
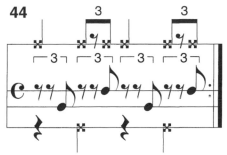
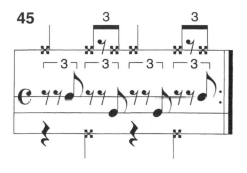

Playing the second partial of the triplet between snare and bass drum (exercises 46-54) can feel awkward at first. Practice with a metronome to avoid rushing the figures. By now, the "shuffle" feel (exercises 55-63) should fall quite naturally between the snare and bass drum.

Various combinations of the previous material are used here, along with the quarter-note-triplet feel between snare and bass drum introduced in exercise 64.

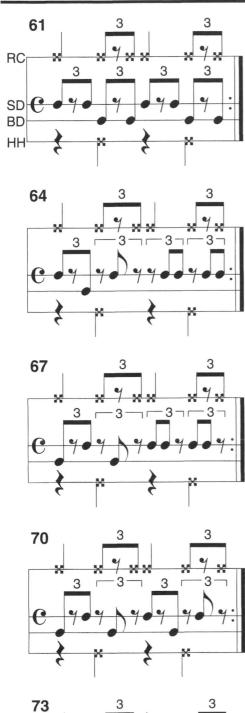
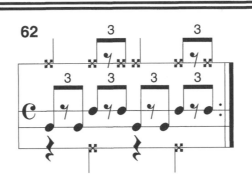
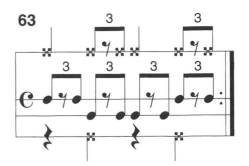
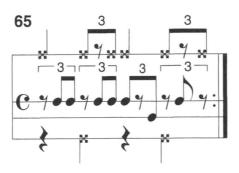
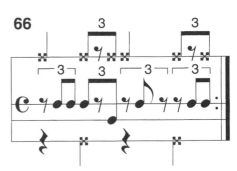
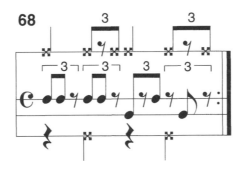
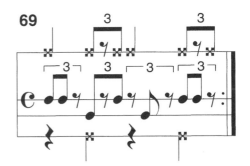
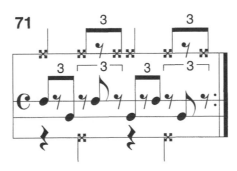
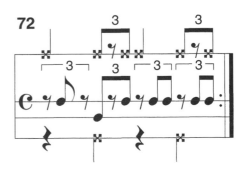

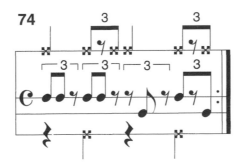
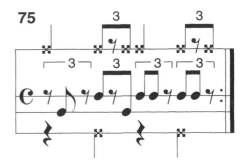

Take ample time with the combination patterns on this page. They present both reading and coordination challenges. Do not move on to Summary Exercises 39 and 40 until you're totally comfortable with all of the one-bar exercises on this page.

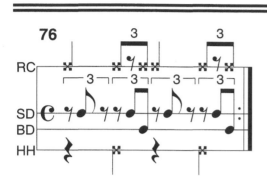

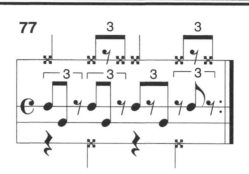

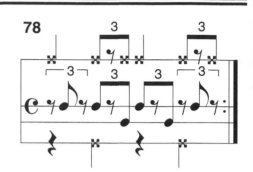

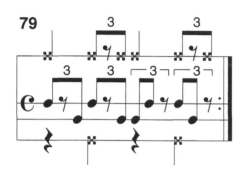

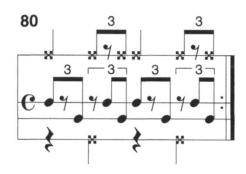

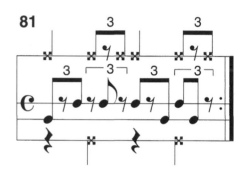

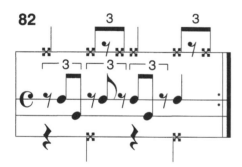

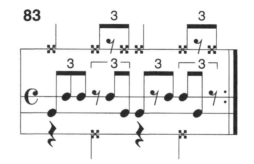

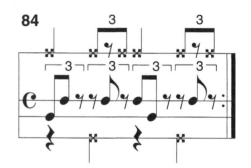

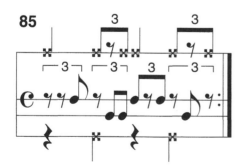

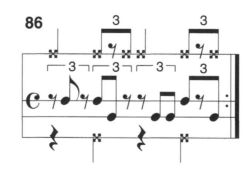

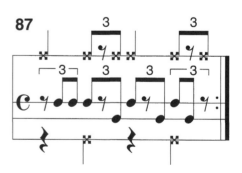

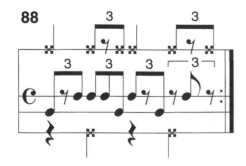

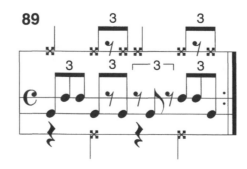

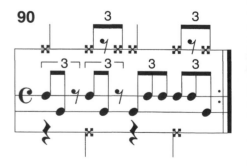

SUMMARY EXERCISE 39

SUMMARY EXERCISE 40

The following six exercises serve as a culmination of everything covered in this book. Quarter notes, 8th notes, syncopated patterns, triplets, and triplet partials between snare drum and bass drum are combined in these studies. Use a metronome (or drum machine), and sing each bar as you play. Do not move on to the next Combination Exercise until you can play the previous one accurately from beginning to end, at different tempos and varied dynamic levels, and with a swinging, relaxed, musical time feel. Most importantly, have *fun* with them.

Exercise 1

Exercise 2

Exercise 3

Exercise 4

Exercise 5

Exercise 6